hRaC

D1490874

the essence of a mother

the essence of a mother
Being Conscious of the Sacred Moments of Motherhood

Julie S. Jensen

Guilford, Connecticut
An imprint of Globe Pequot Press

To buy books in quantity for corporate use
or incentives, call **(800) 962-0973**
or e-mail **premiums@GlobePequot.com.**

Text design: Sheryl Kober
Layout: Maggie Peterson
Project editor: Ellen Urban

Library of Congress Cataloging-in-Publication Data is available on file.

ISBN 978-0-7627-9186-6

Printed in the United States of America

10 9 8 7 6 5 4 3 2 1

For my children,
Scott, McKenna, Abigail, Priscilla, Lola

contents

introduction

The best and most beautiful things in the world cannot be seen or even touched—they must be felt with the heart.

—HELEN KELLER

This book is for you.

Whether you are a single mother or married with children, working mom or stay-at-home mom, a mother of one, two, three, four, or more, have young ones, adolescents, teens, or adult children, have biological or adoptive children, this book is for you. As women, we are here to take care of the children, and every child on the planet is one of our children. We are all here to assist and support one another in taking care of these children. You see, we are all much more alike than we are different. We all want to know we are deeply loved just the way we are. This book is a guide to help our children understand just that. It is vital that our children know without a doubt that because they are here, they matter!

This book is for you!

I have five beautiful, healthy children and a wonderful marriage. At the time of this publishing, my oldest child is my remarkable twenty-two-year-old son, Scott. I am also the mother of four beautiful daughters: McKenna (eighteen), Abigail (fourteen), Priscilla (twelve), and Lola (nine). Not only am I a wife and busy mother of five children, but I also have multiple sclerosis (MS), a debilitating disease that often leaves me bedridden. As my symptoms have progressed, I've naturally asked myself, "What makes a good mother?"

I used to think a good mother was the one who walked into the classroom with impressively decorated homemade cupcakes for her daughter's birthday and cooked healthy, sumptuous meals at a moment's notice, serving them on spotless linens and beautiful dinnerware. She kept a lovely, clean, and organized home, and never failed to escort her kids to and from their many well-rounded activities on time, all the while fully armed with updated schedules, snacks, water, and extra clothes and underwear (you just never know). Aside from looking good and doing well in all areas, from entertaining to staying slim and fit to being philanthropic, this good mother was and would always be a good wife. Did I mention she would always be happy?

No pressure, right? But, as my body has become increasingly disabled, and I can no longer physically keep up with these Herculean undertakings, I have felt my purpose as a mother and my sense of self-worth slip away. I had no choice but to deeply examine my beliefs—the beliefs we all share—and to redefine for myself what makes for a truly "good" mother. If it isn't cupcakes, gourmet meals, decorating, carpooling, and staying beautiful, what is it? What is the *essence* of a mother?

This book contains what I have learned through this transformation—my humble answer to that universal question. We are all on this never-ending journey of growth and discovery. It is my hope that the thoughts shared in this book will linger in your mind long after the words have been read.

It doesn't take a chronic illness or a catastrophe to create awareness. Compassionate, well-intentioned mothers everywhere are caught up in the busyness and *doing* of being a mother, without realizing that they don't have to lose touch with the power they have to be conscious and present, no matter what is going on around them. My life is proof positive that something magical happens when a woman becomes fully aware of her role as a mother. A shift takes place, and she moves naturally from being absorbed in the "doing" to generating life from a place of "be-ing."

I don't know what the future holds for me, but I do believe that my children will thrive. Their foundation has been set, and we are all very grateful. May these tenets—the best of what we've learned in our beautiful family laboratory—have a similar healing effect for you. While my story is unique, the messages contained within it are universal.

It has been difficult for me to feel happy and to have gratitude for my health experience with MS. We are told and expected to show gratitude in all things, and I have always wondered, "How can I be happy and grateful for becoming immobile and disabled?" It took time and many experiences to help me reach a place where I could feel gratitude for my health challenge. First and foremost, MS forced me to slow down. I had an idea of what my future would be like; I imagined a busy lifestyle of cooking healthy meals for my family, being able to run errands, and driving children to activities. However, over time, I was not able to accomplish these tasks, let alone have the dexterity to turn the pages of a book like the one you are now holding. Things as simple as swallowing a drink of water without choking, or taking a deep breath, became challenging, leaving me to spend most of my time in a wheelchair or in bed.

Now, because I am sitting and still for most of my day, my choices are: One, to sit and think, making myself crazy worrying about my situation and what might become of me; or two, to go inward. I have had all of the time needed to be silent and still, praying, meditating, and being available for inspiration. I have felt like I am being replaced, not able to do all the things that I *want* to do. Now, I can see that all along I have been the recipient of, and have always felt, much love and support, so I can do what I really *need* to do. Without this experience, I never would have written this book, nor had the opportunity to touch millions of mothers and their children. I feel like I am the luckiest woman on Earth. I can see now that life has been preparing me all along.

And then the day came,
when the risk
to remain tight
in a bud
was more painful
than the risk
it took
to blossom.

—Anaïs Nin

Now, let's talk about what it takes to create real change in our lives—what I like to call sustainable change.

This is a time in history when it is not enough to simply *know*. It is a time when we have to *know how*, and then we have to apply that knowledge. Words do not teach; only life experience teaches. We are going to test the ideas contained in this book and apply what we learn. We are going to experience what it means to be a conscious mother. When you read a book and collect knowledge, you store it in your brain. It has to become an experience, something you have to demonstrate for your brain to rewire, and then it becomes a part of you. Everything you have learned in life, you have learned through repetition. Talking, walking, riding a bike— it is through practice that we become masters. And so it is with conscious parenting; we will become masters as we apply what we learn and practice. As motivational philosopher Jim Rohn suggests, "You can't hire someone else to do your push-ups for you." We are going to do the hard work ourselves and create lasting, sustainable change.

Anyone who has ever set New Year's resolutions to lose weight, start an exercise program, or quit smoking knows how powerful an existing habit can be. When we do something often, it becomes easy. Most things become easier with practice and repetition, and over time the practice becomes more pleasurable. It is human nature to engage in activities that are pleasurable. So, with practice and repetition, ease and pleasure, we create new habits. Habits seem to be more than just behaviors; they seem to be part of who we are. If you repeat a behavior often enough, the synaptic pathways in the brain get worn in.

In creating sustainable change in our families and parenting styles, I would like to invite you to read one chapter every month. Make it a daily practice to review the chosen chapter and incorporate the suggested exercises every single day for that month. With practice and repetition the new conscious mothering trait will be easier and more pleasurable. It will become a habit.

In his book, *The Success Principles,* Jack Canfield tells the story about a test NASA did several years ago. NASA was testing the psychological and physiological impact of spatial disorientation on potential astronauts. The participants were required to wear convex goggles twenty-four hours a day—without ever taking them off. Everything appeared upside down all of the time. At first, the astronauts were under a lot of stress and anxiety, but eventually they began to adjust. About thirty days into the experiment something amazing happened! The astronauts' brains created new neural pathways, and they started to see everything normally, right side up, even though they were still wearing the convex goggles. NASA repeated the experiment, this time taking off the goggles partway through the experiment. But no new neural pathways had formed. The brain needed thirty uninterrupted, consecutive days for the new neural connections to form. Allow yourself thirty uninterrupted, consecutive days with each chapter to form new neural connections in the brain, creating a new habit.

For us humans, change is uncomfortable. It feels foreign; it feels like something is wrong. But that gives us an opportunity to look at ourselves. Sometimes we might want to quit, we might want to stop, we might want to pull back. You may have heard of Chuck Yeager—the first person in history to break the sound barrier. Recently, I was listening to an interview where he spoke about his flight experience, and he mentioned that the cockpit was in the most turmoil and shook the most right before he broke through the sound barrier. Once he broke through, the flight was the most serene and peaceful he had ever experienced. This is not the beginning of the story, however; prior to Yeager's accomplishment, three different pilots attempted this same feat. But when experiencing the tremendous turbulence, each one became fearful and pulled back, causing the plane to explode. Most times it is uncomfortable and even downright terrifying to create change in our lives. But just like Chuck Yeager's flight, if we can work through the turbulence and uncomfortable times in life, what is waiting on the other side is peaceful and serene.

It may seem daunting as we try to make not just change but *sustainable* change in our lives. To make this important point, we can look to an interesting discovery in meteorology called the butterfly effect. In 1961, Edward Norton Lorenz entered a figure for wind velocity into a computer to predict weather conditions. In taking a shortcut, he entered .506 instead of .506127. What he discovered was astounding: The minuscule difference of .000127 significantly altered the developing weather pattern. The concept around this finding became known as the butterfly effect, because the seemingly insignificant change in wind velocity of .000127 is similar to the wind velocity caused by the flapping wings of a butterfly. Lorenz concluded that the most insignificant change in the initial condition could drastically affect the weather condition going forward. This slight variation could cause such a meteorological effect that it could change what would be a sunny day into a tornado.

A tiny shift matters that much. As we look at making changes in our lives, we must remember—just as in the atmosphere—every small variable can make a significant and influential impact. We are the direct source of our experience in life, and by making small shifts and changes in how we show up as mothers, we can significantly influence those around us in positive ways.

Be the change you wish to see in the world.

— Mahatma Gandhi

one

A conscious mother . . . takes 100 percent radical self-responsibility.

In the long run, we shape our lives, and we shape ourselves. The process never ends until we die. And the choices we make are ultimately our own responsibility.

—ELEANOR ROOSEVELT

If you could kick the person in the pants responsible for most of your trouble, you wouldn't sit for a month.

—THEODORE ROOSEVELT

The Roosevelts had it right. They knew the importance of taking self-responsibility and the influence that it can have on your life. When finalizing the manuscript for *The Essence of a Mother,* I posed a simple question on Facebook: What are some of the challenges and obstacles you face as a parent? The challenges were varied and interesting—from co-parenting with an ex-spouse to allowing free agency for your children in making their own choices, to finding time to parent when working. My reason for asking the question was to be sure that this book would touch on a wide variety of obstacles we face as parents. Although the question is simple, I find that the answers can be quite complex.

For sure, we do not always have all of the answers, but when we look at taking 100 percent radical self-responsibility, we as mothers are no longer victims; instead, we become the victors in any situation. We are not able to control every situation or other people's behavior, but we can always control how we will react, respond, and behave. I may not be able to control my health situation, but I can control how I will show up every day. Picture this: If I were to wake up every morning feeling sorry for myself, grumpy, depressed, and impatient, can you imagine what kind of scenario this would create in my life? I am certain my husband and children would not enjoy my company and would avoid being in my presence. Conversely, if I choose to wake up every morning extending love, patience, and gratitude, my life will reflect something much different. I am positive my friends and family will enjoy spending time with me.

There are a few actions that are an essential part of taking 100 percent radical self-responsibility. First, it is important to acknowledge that *you* are solely responsible for the choices in your life. I mentioned earlier that we cannot always control the situation we are in, but we can take full responsibility for our reactions, behavior, and thoughts. Here is the tip for controlling your thoughts: When you have a bad thought, acknowledge it and say to yourself, "Well, that was unpleasant and unnecessary." We really do not need to have unpleasant thoughts. We are responsible for what we choose to feel and think.

Second, you cannot blame others for the choices you have made. I once had an acquaintance who had a very difficult time taking self-responsibility. He was always blaming others for the problems in his life. He would even go so far as to blame his second-grade teacher for why he was unhappy. When we realize that we are the source of our own happiness, we can take steps to create greater levels of peace and happiness for ourselves.

Third, you have to recognize that you are your own best cheerleader. It is not reasonable or healthy to depend on others to make you feel good about yourself. If we allow our happiness to lie outside of ourselves, we will continually be disappointed. We tap into our own personal power when we realize that we are in control of feeling good about ourselves.

Fourth, you have to own up to your own mistakes. It is easy to pass the buck and blame someone else when we make a mistake. Recently, this type of behavior became common among heads of the nation's largest corporations and banks when they testified before Congress as to their role— or, rather, lack thereof—in the collapse of the US economy. They only stated that "mistakes were made," and yet failed to name anything specific for which they may have been personally at fault. With this type of "pass the buck" behavior, it is nearly impossible to correct and change the situation. We have seen multiple problems in the global economy, and today's generation (fondly referred to as Millennials) has witnessed bailout after bailout. No one is taking responsibility for the problems at hand, and everyone is waiting for someone else to step up and rescue them. When we realize that no one is coming, it liberates us to take action and responsibility in all areas of our lives. When we understand this, it helps us to become more self-reliant, and to realize our responsibility for how our lives turn out.

After the *Columbia* space shuttle explosion, which killed seven astronauts, launch integration manager N. Wayne Hale Jr. said, "I had the opportunity and information and I failed to make use of it. I don't know what an inquest for a court of law would say, but I stand condemned in the court of my own conscience to be guilty of not preventing the *Columbia* disaster. . . . The bottom line is that I failed to understand what I was being told; I failed to stand up and be counted. Therefore, look no further; I am guilty of allowing the *Columbia* to crash." The outright honesty of Mr. Hale in taking full responsibility for his failures is striking, especially because statements like this are rare nowadays. It is all too common to justify our failures to one degree or another. Taking full responsibility for our shortcomings requires humility and courage, both very desirable human traits.

Here is something to think about: If you squeeze an orange, what comes out? Orange juice. And why is that? Because that is what's inside—orange juice. Now, let's relate this to you: If someone "squeezes" you or makes you upset, what comes out? Anger, hatred, or love? What is inside of you? I shared this analogy with my youngest daughter, asking her what comes out when you squeeze an orange. Her answer was orange juice, of course. Then I asked her if someone squeezed her, or made her mad, what would come out? She responded without hesitation: hatred. We had a conversation about how she could be responsible for what comes out of her, no matter what the conduct of other people might be. If someone at school gives her a cross look, or her sisters are impatient with her, *she can choose* to respond in a positive way so she can create more peace in her life. I helped her to see how her behavior would affect how she felt. This can be tricky to do, but with practice it becomes easier. We have a common saying in our home when we feel like someone has treated us badly: "It's a good thing we don't allow other people's poor behavior to affect how we feel and how we respond."

Exercises for taking 100 percent radical self-responsibility:

- When facing a challenge with your child, have the humility and courage to look at your own life and how you may have contributed to the situation.

- As Maya Angelou so astutely said, "If you don't like something, change it. If you can't change it, change your attitude." By applying this quote to your own life, you have the ability to affect the outcome in every situation.

- The only person you can control is you. Once you've acknowledged that you're the one who chooses your responses and behaviors, you'll be in full control of your life.

- Listen to the voices in your head. Eliminate blame and excuses, and this will shift the responsibility solely to you. Teach your children to do this as well.

two

A conscious mother . . .
values being together.

Piglet sidled up to Pooh from behind. "Pooh?" he whispered.
"Yes, Piglet?"
"Nothing," said Piglet, taking Pooh's hand. "I just wanted to be
sure of you."

—A. A. MILNE, *WINNIE-THE-POOH*

One morning, I was having an off day and needed rest. I found it difficult to move, or even to get out of bed. My limbs felt heavy, and every part of me ached with exhaustion. I decided to honor my body and remain tucked cozily under my covers. In the quiet of my room, my daughter Priscilla peeked in and asked if she could lay in bed with me and keep me company. I wanted to be still and sleep; I wanted to be alone. Priscilla wanted to be together, and when I looked at her sweet, round face, her tan, ten-year-old skin, and all the innocence, sweetness, and hope in her eyes, it sucked me right in.

"Can I come in?" she asked.

"Of course!" I replied.

I stayed motionless and she climbed up on the bed, snuggled beside me, and launched into a long and passionate story of the playground game, four square. She told me who she played with during recess and what strategies she used to beat them. She talked about how to bounce the ball in the square next to hers, or how to send it kitty-corner across the pavement.

I found myself thinking about how my body was exhausted and how I wanted to be alone. And quickly, I realized that in thinking about myself, I was not truly listening to her. *Get over yourself, Julie,* I thought. *Be here with her. She needs you.* I shifted my focus and listened intently to Priscilla as she went from four square to tetherball, and whom she played with in that game, why she liked it, and the strategies she used there to win.

Priscilla: "Mom, I love tetherball, and I'm really good."

Me (fully listening, being a witness to her young life): "Wow, honey! That's great. I was really good at tetherball when I was your age, too."

Priscilla: "You were? I am just like you." She was beaming.

From there, Priscilla moved the conversation swiftly to her knee socks. Tall and white and part of her school uniform, the silly things kept falling down, slouching toward her ankles at the most inopportune times.

"When we're in the middle of a game, I have to stop and pull them up," she said exasperated. "I think I need a different size. What do you think?"

I told her she was right—that we would find different socks that fit better and stayed right where they were supposed to be at all times.

Priscilla looked happy and we fell into an easy silence. I could feel her small, warm body, just beside me. For a few moments, she seemed content, as if she had finished telling me all the important pieces of her life.

Suddenly, I saw her face light up, as if lit from within. She remembered one more important piece. "Mom," she said, "I just *love* spending time with you."

I was lying there like a lump on the bed and she was happy—overjoyed, even—just to *be* with me. She was absolutely beaming. She didn't need me to be "doing" all of the things we make ourselves busy with, such as running errands, shopping, cleaning the house, finishing homework, making dinner, and so on; she was happy just *being* with me.

Her love radiated out and warmed me, too. I was overjoyed.

If I had stayed inside my own head, listening to my thoughts and tuning her out, I would have felt inadequate—unable to accomplish everything that I thought a good and responsible mom should be doing. And if I had stayed in my thoughts, I would have felt that I *was* inadequate. In my previous hectic, "healthy," and mobile life, I would have been focused on making sure I had the perfect afterschool snack on a pretty plate, ready and waiting to be gobbled up, so we could rush off and be on time to the next extracurricular activity. I am not purporting that these little details are not important, or that they are unappreciated; what I have learned is that they are secondary to just *being* with our children.

When I chose to listen completely to Priscilla—to be fully present for her—I was more than adequate. She simply wanted to spend time with me, even when I was feeling paralyzed and stuck. She was sharing her ten-year-old life with me, and she was happy just *being with me.*

The Importance of Listening When Being with Our Children

Whenever my children are talking to me, instead of thinking about what's going on around me or how I'm going to reply, I make a conscious effort to really listen. I hang on every word as if it is the most important message my child is ever going to say to me. I try to communicate like this with my husband, too. Whether he is talking about Kobe Bryant and the Lakers or *Finding Bigfoot,* both of which I don't have much interest in, I listen all the same. Basketball and Bigfoot are important to him. It is important that he feels heard, and that he feels like he has a deep connection with me. We have that bond because I stay present. It's the connection anyone can have with another human being by just *being* together.

I talk to my kids about listening; just listening. As parents, we are models of behavior for our children, and when they see us truly being attentive to those who are speaking, it teaches them to respect what others have to say. When I talked with my children about how to listen to another person with this amount of interest and attention, my oldest daughter McKenna tried it, and it changed her experience in school.

"I was listening to a teacher that I normally get bored with," she told me. "I tried listening to her in the new way you taught me. And I hate to say it, but I felt a closeness to my teacher; I totally did. I understood and remembered what she said. That really, really worked. Thank you, Mom."

As parents, we get busy. We are always multitasking— making dinner, or thinking about whose homework still needs to get done, the bills that need to be paid, and who needs a bath, all the while talking to our children. We respond, "Yeah, yeah, tetherball, sure," and we miss the importance of that child's life, an opportunity to be a witness to the beauty of another's journey. So often kids just really want our attention. They couldn't care less about all the little things we fuss over, but they feel valued, appreciated, and worthy when we give them our undivided attention and they see that we are making eye contact and earnestly listening to what they have to say.

As we spend time just being with our children, and they know that we are attentive and deeply listening, we build a foundation of trust. Our children will know that they can turn to us for anything, big or small, and we will be there for them, without judgment. It is always important that our children know we are there for them, but this is especially important as they grow older, and they feel the struggles in their lives are more difficult to navigate. We always want our children to feel safe confiding in us.

Studies show that when children form a close bond with their mother, they are more likely to perform better in school and have fewer behavioral problems. This close bond with their mother also increases their emotional intelligence, helping them to be successful in future relationships. It has long been known that good parent-teen communication can help to lessen the influence of negative peer pressure. But new research shows that it is a child's mother who is the most influential when it comes to her child's decision making about alcohol, drugs, and sex. Some researchers speculate that the nature of mother-child communication accounts for the difference: Mothers usually don't have one big "drug talk" or "sex talk," but instead tend to weave the topic into multiple conversations or family activities.

When Priscilla was talking about playground games and knee socks, it was the most important thing for her, right then. I could honor that, and honor her, by listening. We were simply *being* together. There is something magical about just *being*. In a busy and chaotic world, our children look to us for that calm, soothing place. Many times we feel we are too busy to just pause, pay attention, and *be*.

In 2009 the Commissioner for Children and Young People embarked on research into children and young people's views on their well-being. The research revealed that acknowledgment and independence were important contributors to their well-being. Being listened to, having their views respected, and being involved in decisions affecting them were seen as important aspects of their well-being.

Children want to know that the adults in their lives are acknowledging the things that are important to them. When we listen to our kids and include them in making decisions for the family, they feel valued, respected, and appreciated.

Whenever we decide to make time for the experience of stillness in our lives . . . it is like a basin of silty water that's all muddy and you let it sit on the table until the silt sinks to the bottom of the basin, and then you have clear water at the top . . . and that is what stillness is.

—Reverend Ed Bacon

Finding Moments of Stillness in Busy Family Schedules

Mornings can be a tough time to find stillness. They are usually a busy time for most families with children: waking up, getting dressed, making sure the backpack is together, having breakfast, and remembering the school lunch. For our family, with two adults and five schoolchildren, that is seven breakfasts and five lunches—twelve meals before we leave the house in the morning.

When I was healthy, I was right there, overseeing all of it. Commandeering the kitchen, I made breakfasts and lunches and checked backpacks. I helped my youngest daughter Lola make sure her uniform was ready to go, and ensured that the others were on task and prepared for the day ahead.

Now, mornings are the most difficult time of the day for me. I have worried, "How can I get up and be productive? How can I help my children be prepared for their days?" And the truth is, many days I can't—not in the same way I once did. Most mornings, I need help to get out of bed, use the bathroom, and get dressed and ready for the day. It may take me two to three hours to get up, get ready, and get out the door. My heart is willing, but my body doesn't cooperate. I feel frustrated that I cannot "do" more. Then I remember that the most important thing I can do for my children is to *be* with them. No matter what our life circumstances—stay-at-home mom, working mother, healthy, sick, tired, or rested—we can *always* make space for just *being* with our children.

I can be there. I can listen. And I have learned that I need to. It's not okay for me to stay in bed and sleep when they're going off to school. My youngest daughter mentioned to me that she feels better about her day and more secure going to school when I am just *being* with her while she gets ready for the day.

So I get up and sit in my wheelchair. My children take care of everything to get themselves ready, and sometimes they help me, so I can just be there. Once I started doing this, I could see the difference it made. Lola was so happy. There was a noticeable change in her behavior. When I was lying in bed, she wondered if I was okay. She worried. When I just sat up in bed or sat in my wheelchair, she felt much more confident and ready to leave the house.

We mothers can take a load off ourselves. We can stop fretting and micromanaging the minute details of each lunch bag and focus on the bigger picture. We can really, really be present with our children. Our children will feel the difference. Being a "good" mother is about so much more than *doing*—it's about *being* there for our children when they need our undivided attention, listening, and giving them the security of knowing we are there for them.

Being Attentive

As mothers, we get busy with a multitude of things we want to accomplish on any given day. Sometimes when our children talk to us, we act like we're listening with a swift nod of the head in agreement. Or a quick "Yes, honey," when we (and they) know that we didn't hear a single word they just said. Listen to your child when she is speaking to you. Listen as though it is the most important thing she will ever share with you in her lifetime. You'll notice that you will connect with your child on a deeper level, and that your child will feel validated and loved.

The message we are giving our children when we don't spend quality time just being with them is that they are not important. When we are busy answering the phone, getting things done, or thinking that what we have to do tomorrow is more important than being with our children in the present moment, they get the message loud and clear: Being with them and truly knowing them is not a priority to us. Ask yourself if you are too busy to just *be* with your child. Are you too busy to know about your child's thoughts and feelings? Do you have time to just play with or hang out with your child? While we might tell our children they are loved, they will not feel it if we don't take the time to just be with them. Words don't cut it when actions don't follow. Our children need our focused attention. The simple act of being attentive and fully present with our children will do more for them than we could ever imagine. We have opportunities each day, even if for a small amount of time, to fully cherish our children by just *being* with them.

Have you ever been visiting with someone and as you are talking, she responds to a text message or starts browsing through her e-mail? When we do this, it takes us away from being with whomever we are with. It makes us feel ignored or unimportant to the person we are with. Sometimes when we're sitting on the couch as a family, my kids' phones light up with a text message. It takes them away—even though in our family, when we're together, we have chosen not to respond immediately to text messages. Our guideline is simple: If you're talking to real human being, the pixels on your phone don't count as real. Humans first, pixels second.

With our busy schedules, it can be challenging to find quality, one-on-one time with our children. I have found that if I don't schedule it on my calendar, it's not "real," or it won't happen. So, I have a standing special date with my youngest daughter on Tuesday evening, from seven to eight p.m. I have it marked on my calendar. Most of the time it's as simple as playing a game, coloring a picture, or going out for an ice cream cone or a hot chocolate. Even on a Tuesday evening, when I don't have much energy for anything, I still make time just for Lola. A couple of times we have simply snuggled in bed together, watching TV or reading a book. I make a point to let everyone know that I am not available from seven to eight p.m. I will not answer a phone call or a text message, and if someone wanting to tell me something interrupts us, I let them know I will get back to them after eight o'clock. Lola will quickly interject, "Don't intrude on my time with Mom." She can count on me being alone with her for that one hour, every Tuesday night.

On our last date, Lola observed and commented, "Mom, you know why you're a really great date?"

Me, flattered by the compliment: "Why?"

Lola: "Because you don't talk on the phone when we're together."

It is critical to Lola that we have our special time together, just the two of us. Excuses may creep in, such as "I don't have enough money or the time to do something spectacular." Don't allow these silly excuses to stop you from being with your child. Lola really doesn't care about what we are doing, the simple or the extravagant, the costly or the free. The most important thing for her is that I am simply being with her, and that she can count on that time with me.

This does not necessarily work for my adolescent and teenage children. Spending time with just Mom, or having a standing date with me, is "dorky." With my older children, I take special note of the items, friends, and activities that are interesting to them at the moment. Then, I try to enter their world, ask them questions, and get them talking about their lives. I'll say something like, "I've noticed you like to Snapchat. How does that work? Tell me about it." Or, "What is something fun you would like to do this month? Let's talk about it and make it happen." I am always pleasantly surprised at how much my otherwise "quiet, introverted" adolescent daughter will share when we're talking about her and what's going on in her world. Most people really enjoy talking about themselves, including our children.

The True Meaning of "Being"

Now that we have discussed *being*, let's dissect the definition. Webster defines it as the quality or state of having existence;

something conceivable as existing; conscious existence. *Conscious existence* is being fully aware of one's state or reality.

At first glance, the act of being may seem like doing nothing, but it is actually a very active way of life. As we practice being, we find that we are more engaged in the moment, and we activate a heightened awareness of our feelings and needs, as well as those of the people around us.

On June 23, 2013, daredevil Nik Wallenda accomplished one of the greatest feats known to mankind. He became the first man to walk across the Grand Canyon on a tightrope. Without any harnesses or safety precautions, Nik was suspended fifteen hundred feet above the ground (about fifty feet higher than the Empire State Building) and walked the length of five football fields while balancing on a two-inch-thick wire. To accomplish this record-breaking feat, Nik Wallenda had to be completely present. He had to be in a radical state of being. If Nik had lost focus for one second, his life would have been over. I'm not suggesting that losing focus and not "being" with our children is a matter of life and death, but I am suggesting that we should make it a point to have that same radical state of being when interacting with our children. Our children will understand how magnificent, important, and precious they are just by our being with them. They will know that because they are here, they matter . . . period.

Today I learned an interesting piece of trivia. According to Google's Eric Schmidt, we humans create the equivalent amount of information in just two days that we created from the beginning of civilization up through the year 2003. We are on information overload, big-time. Let me repeat that: The amount of information created from the dawn of human civilization through the year 2003 is equal to the amount of information we now generate in just two days. As mothers, we must make an effort to cut through the clutter and manage the amount and type of information that is entering our home every day.

I see this as a potential problem when I observe my children *constantly* on their smartphones and other technology gadgets. There is continual distraction as their phones light up with group text messages, Snapchat, Instagram, and other forms of social media. It is becoming more and more challenging for my children to be still and just be. Upon researching the effects on the development of the brain, I have learned that the constant stream of stimulation has a major effect on distorting the pleasure center of the brain. It is no longer enough to walk the dog, visit with Grandma, or sit and watch the sunset with the family. These simple pleasures in life are now "too slow" and "too boring." We must provide an example to our children of the enjoyment and satisfaction that comes with just being. We cannot leave this training to society. If we do, our children will continue to be overloaded with information, missing out on the sweetness of knowing how to just be—with themselves, and with others.

Exercises for being with your child:

- Take a moment to stop and sit with your child or loved one. Just visit. Stay completely focused on the person right in front of you. Love and relationship expert Katherine Woodward Thomas has said, "The currency of love is attention." *Be* with your child, give him consideration, and fill his "love bank account" with the currency of your attention.

- Turn off all technology for just thirty minutes each day. Just *be*. Sit and relish the silence. You will enjoy the present moment without interruption from the outside world.

- When you are saying good-bye to your children before they leave your home and step out into the world for the day, be completely present to them as you send them off. Look them in the eye and say each of their names. They will enter the world with confidence, feeling their mother's love.

- If you have a large family and find it difficult to give each child your undivided attention, set aside particular days or times each week when you will do something special together, one on one—whether it's just reading a story or sitting and visiting.

- Listen to your child with complete attention and presence. Listen as though it is the most important thing she will ever say, or listen as though she is sharing the last words she will ever speak in her lifetime. I promise that you will feel a closer connection with your child, and your child will feel a closer connection with you. Could a mother ask for anything more? Beautiful!

three

A conscious mother . . .
provides opportunities for her children
to develop self-reliance.

This above all: to thine own self be true.

—WILLIAM SHAKESPEARE

You can empower your children by allowing them to figure out how to do things in their own, unique way. This helps our children to develop self-reliance and honor their own sense of discernment. We each come to Earth with an inner knowledge of our unique purpose. Deep inside we know, and age does not make a difference as to when we understand this purpose. Give your children opportunities to make decisions for themselves and learn to trust their own inner guidance system.

Here is a simple illustration of how I allow my young children to practice making their own choices and realizing their own preferences. One evening when it was time to prepare for the next day, I said to my three young daughters, "If I was getting ready for school, I would . . ." and proceeded to suggest what I would do: take a bath; brush my teeth; lay out my uniform, shoes, and backpack; pack my lunch. Then I let them decide what they needed to do to prepare for school the following morning.

They each had their own unique way of going about preparing for school. Lola, my youngest, decided that it was not important for her to take a bath. Instead, it was important for her to make sure her pencil pouch was organized and in her backpack. It was important for her to have her running shoes packed because she knew she had PE the next day.

Abi, who was in seventh grade, knew she would feel most confident if she was organized and well put together. It was important for her to take a shower, wash and blow-dry her hair, curl it, and set out her makeup. She wanted to know her homework was finished, organized, and in her backpack exactly as she would need it the next day. She needed to have the right paper in the right folder for each class, so she would be completely prepared and organized when she arrived at school.

Priscilla, my fifth grader, had an entirely different agenda. For her, it was most important to have a delicious and healthy lunch packed. Her first priority was to walk downstairs to the kitchen and make a Caprese salad. She cut the tomatoes, basil, and mozzarella cheese and put some balsamic dressing in a little container, so she would have a delicious, beautiful lunch the next day. Then she came back upstairs and laid out her uniform and put together her backpack.

Each child had a different approach to getting ready, none of them wrong. Each of them knew what was important for them to feel prepared to be successful for their day. Who am I to say that taking a shower and washing your hair first are more important than packing your lunch? They knew what they needed to do to be prepared for their day. The next morning, they were each ready for school, and on time!

By allowing them to get ready themselves, they learned self-reliance. Give children an opportunity to decide for themselves what to do. It allows them to exercise that muscle of validating their own discernment, and to have the experience of knowing that they can make smart choices for themselves. By "exercising that muscle" on the little decisions, like getting ready for school each day, they learn to trust their judgment when making "bigger" decisions.

Avoid Being a Helicopter Parent

Have you heard the term *helicopter parent?* A helicopter parent is one that hovers closely over her children, ensuring that they make the right decisions, and will swoop down at her children's slightest sign of discomfort or pain. She is there to help save the day, taking away the great opportunity of making a mistake and learning from it. Helicopter parents are overly involved in their children's experiences and problems. Most children enjoy having helicopter parents, because they know their parents will do just about anything for them. A child of a helicopter parent learns that she does not have to be responsible for her life because her helicopter parent will swoop in and make everything all right.

For example, a child goes to school, forgetting her water bottle, only to call her mother, asking her to bring the water bottle down to the school. A helicopter parent will hop in the car and bring the water bottle right over. A powerful parent is interested in teaching self-reliance and will say, "Oh, honey, I'm sorry you forgot your water. That must stink! Well, at least you can use the school drinking fountain, so you don't pass out from dehydration. See you when you get home from school. I love you."

Now, which child do you think will remember her water bottle in the future?

Ask yourself, am I helping or hovering?

When I was four years old, my preschool class obtained an incubator and several chicken eggs. Every day we would anxiously check the incubator to see if the chicks had hatched. It was difficult to be patient. After several days of waiting, one of my preschool classmates had an idea to speed up the hatching process: "Once the beak pecks through the shell, we can help the chicks get out faster by peeling off the shell." Our teacher overheard the plan and stepped in, telling us that if the chick did not work hard to peck his way out of the shell by himself, he would die. The hard struggle of breaking through the shell made the chick strong and resilient, and much better prepared for life. When we allow our children to work through difficult times and figure out a solution, they too become stronger and more resilient.

Building Self-Reliance Will Help Your Child Tackle Life's Big Decisions

When my sixteen-year-old daughter McKenna was struggling to decide between two extracurricular activities, I encouraged her to trust her own decision. She could have continued her participation with a fun-filled, touring performance youth group, or she could have left that group and chosen to develop her dancing talents by working one-on-one with a professional ballroom dancing instructor. It was a tough choice, because both options had their advantages.

The performing group traveled to fun places; McKenna went to Peru one summer, to Taiwan another, and she would have been headed to China the following summer if she decided to tour with them. McKenna loved the travel and loved her friends in the group, but she was also feeling that the training wasn't rigorous enough to develop her talents as a dancer. All of her friends were in this group, and when she told them she was considering leaving, they gave her a hard time about it. "Oh, you think you're better than our group," they said. "You have to go with a professional. You're really going to miss out."

McKenna struggled with her choices and came to me one afternoon to talk about it. "Mom, I'm confused," she said. "I feel unclear about the direction I should go. What do you think I should do?"

She was looking for me to give her the answer, and I could have. I could have said, "You should stick with your friends; forget the ballroom dancing." Or I could have said,

"Do the ballroom dancing; leave your friends." Whatever I suggested, she would have followed. She trusts me, as her mother, and thinks I know the perfect solution. In this case, I knew she could figure out the answer, too, and wanted her to find it on her own. I wanted to give her the opportunity to think about her situation, make a choice, and either fail or succeed. This would help McKenna learn to trust her own sense of discernment when the stakes were a little higher than getting ready for school, but still low if she were to make a poor choice.

I didn't think she could make a serious mistake choosing between extracurricular activities. It wasn't like she was thirty and trying to decide on a career or who to marry. Those are big life-changing decisions, and this was merely a choice between two opportunities to dance. The stakes seemed high to McKenna, but in the big picture, they weren't necessarily life-altering. Because of that, it was not hard for me to listen to her explain the situation, hear her confusion, and choose not to offer a solution, giving her the gift of knowing she could figure out the perfect solution, herself.

McKenna loved participating in the performing group with all of her friends. At the same time, she didn't feel she was reaching her full potential as a dancer. She wanted and needed more specific training in dance and performing. I listened to McKenna and encouraged her to take some time to think, pray, go within, and find the answer. She followed my recommendations and came up with the perfect solution: She decided not to follow the crowd, but to follow her own heart and study ballroom dancing with the professional. McKenna missed seeing her friends from the group, but she really committed herself to her dance training, and saw it pay off. She entered dance competitions and wound up placing first in every dance she competed in. Her Latin ballroom training has paid off; she is now eighteen, and has become a fitness instructor teaching a Latin dance workout. She enjoys it, and she is an excellent instructor because of her early training. When she made the decision as a sixteen-year-old, she didn't know what the ultimate impact would be. She just knew she was following her heart. Fast-forward two years: Because of her dance training, she is having fun and starting a career she loves while attending college.

McKenna learned a priceless lesson—that she can rely on her own power of discernment and know that she will be guided to the perfect solution. I did not need to give her the solution to her problem; she came up with an answer that worked perfectly for her.

Everyone is a genius. But if you judge a fish on its ability to climb a tree, it will spend its whole life believing it is stupid.

—*Albert Einstein*

Allow children to discover the gift of their own discernment and become more self-reliant. Each of us has all of the information we need to make an accurate evaluation, assessment, and choice. Give your children the opportunity to ask questions and work things out by themselves. I believe that this is one of the most important things we can teach our children. If they trust their own judgment, they will not second-guess any decision they have to make in their lives. When our children are out in the world and we are not there to guide them, they will know what it feels like to make a choice, find a solution, and honor their own discernment. And if we teach them how to do this at a young age, they will be better at trusting their own judgment when making more-important life decisions, such as where to attend college, which career path they should follow, or who they want to marry someday.

As for McKenna, her ability to trust her inner knowing paid off almost immediately. When she was seventeen, her classmates honored her by selecting her to be the homecoming queen at her school. For the homecoming dance, a group of forty kids were going together, and McKenna was set up on a blind date with a boy from another school. As they were planning their date—asking each other what to wear, and what color corsage to buy—they were getting to know each other.

He started saying things to her that made her uncomfortable. He asked questions she felt were inappropriate—*Have you kissed a guy? What more would you do?*—in a roundabout way, trying to be funny, but also feeling out exactly where McKenna was, where he stood, and what might happen on their blind date. When she didn't answer the way he hoped, he started making fun of her for her moral standards. She was beginning to feel more and more uncomfortable as the date of the dance drew near.

The Friday night before the dance, McKenna attended the homecoming football game where she was crowned queen. The next morning, she went to school to help decorate for the dance. She kept having the feeling that she shouldn't go with her blind date. You know that feeling you get inside, when you just know something isn't right? Sometimes we listen to that feeling and sometimes we ignore it, brushing it off like we are being silly. In his book *The Gift of Fear,* Gavin de Becker encourages us to tune into that feeling: "Like every creature, you can know when you are in the presence of danger [or just an off situation]. You have the gift of a brilliant, internal guardian that stands ready to warn you of hazards and guide you through risky situations." We need to teach our children to listen to that feeling.

McKenna didn't want to go out with someone who made fun of her, and she didn't want to feel pressured to do something she didn't want to do. She decided to follow her heart and honor her own sense of discernment. So she called up her date and said, "You have been rude to me, and I would rather go to the dance alone than go with someone who's capable of being rude and disrespectful to me."

That night, McKenna showered, dressed, and applied her makeup. She bought her own corsage, got in her car, and drove to the school alone, got out of her car alone, and walked into the dance alone. Around three thousand students attend her school, and most students went to the homecoming dance. All eyes were on McKenna as she walked in all by herself. Other students asked, "Where's your date? Why are you here alone?" But she didn't care. She knew she would rather attend the dance alone than be with someone who could disrespect her.

I was so proud of her, and happy that she had the confidence in herself to make a good choice. And she had a fabulous time. When she returned home, she said jokingly, "I don't think I will ever go to a dance with a date again. I had so much fun."

The entire school was there supporting her and cheering for her. It really worked out. She was able to be an example to all the other kids. By her actions and by following her heart, she showed her peers that they can follow their inner guidance system, too. If any of the other girls didn't want to drink or fool around with boys, McKenna encouraged them to stand up and say no. "I didn't go to the dance with someone who was mean to me," she said. "You don't have to go to a party with alcohol and drugs if it doesn't feel right to you."

McKenna listened to her heart. I wasn't there with her to say, "Don't go with him; this isn't right." She just knew the familiar feeling of being self-reliant and trusting her own intuition. If you follow your heart, it will never lead you astray. Inside each of us is all of the information we need to make an accurate evaluation.

Providing Opportunities for Self-Reliance

By allowing our children to be self-reliant and honor their sense of discernment, they learn to trust their intuition. It really is a gift, an internal guidance system.

There are many ways we can encourage self-reliance within our children. From the time our children are very young, there are many opportunities for them to learn self-reliance, and it is vitally important for their development to learn that value. For example, a baby can learn self-reliance through its ability to self-soothe when upset. Young children can learn self-reliance when we give them the option of choice, such as, "Would you rather wear the blue shirt or the red shirt?" We can encourage our children to complete tasks on their own. For our young children, it may be tying a shoe or folding laundry; for our older children, that task may be cooking a meal or finishing a big homework assignment. Sure, we can accomplish these tasks more quickly and efficiently than our children, but we take away their opportunity to learn these important life skills if we step in and do it for them. We also take away their ability to be creative and use their problem-solving skills. Remember, they, too, have been endowed with an internal guidance system. As we allow our children to accomplish tasks on their own, they will surely become better with each effort, mistake, and success. Remember to praise your children for their efforts and let them know that even adults fail and make mistakes, especially when attempting a task for the first time. It is all part of the process.

When driving our car we can put a destination in the GPS system and it will give us the correct route to arrive at the exact location entered. If we make a wrong turn, the GPS system will quickly give us an alternate route so we can get back on track. Our internal guidance system is similar. If we just listen to the directions given by our internal guidance system, we will be given the correct route to arrive exactly where we need to be in life. Notice I said *need* to be in life, not *want* to be in life.

Our children are relying on us to teach them how to approach the world. Sometimes that means watching and learning from us, and other times that means we need to watch and encourage them to figure it out on their own.

One of my good friends from high school, Kelly, shared with me a beautiful story of how she honored her own discernment and intuition regarding her daughter's health situation:

Jaylene started seventh grade on July 22. The week prior to beginning her junior high career, she started to become anxious, extremely sensitive, and very "clingy" to me. On the first day of school, Jaylene woke up saying she had a terrible stomachache, but I told her she had to go to school, strongly believing that once she got to school and saw her friends, she would calm down and feel better.

Unfortunately, within three hours or so, I received a call from the school stating that Jaylene was in the nurse's office with a stomachache and a low-grade fever. Her pain wouldn't go away, so I took her to the doctor. The pain was so horrific that the doctor decided to admit her to Children's Hospital. No one could help her in the hospital, and by day seven, Jaylene was worse. At this point, the psych team was sent in for a psychological evaluation. I was livid. As her mother, I knew this was not psychological, and if someone would just watch her try to get out of bed, examine her, take some additional images, I knew that they would find something. The "experts" just dismissed me as the "overprotective, high-strung" mother.

After getting some very confusing information pre-
sented to us by several different doctors, a pain manage-
ment team, a psychiatric team, and a half-dozen student
doctors, Jaylene was sent home on day eight, unable to
walk due to horrible pain, being told that they believed her
pain was part mental and part physical. They labeled her
release papers with "anxiety" and "functional abdominal
pain." They sent us home with six or seven different medi-
cations, told me to increase her Prozac, and to get her in to
see a therapist right away.

Long story short, this continued for three weeks, with
Jaylene in and out of the hospital and having multiple
doctors' visits. I finally was fed up. My daughter was in ex-
cruciating pain and nothing was helping her; the pain was
getting worse. So, I put my foot down, decided to listen to
what my heart was telling me, and guide the doctors to follow my gut feeling. They did, and we found that the horrific
pain was caused by a simple problem: constipation.

Once I'd honored my own discernment and inner
knowing, we were able to move forward with helping my
daughter. Immediately the pain was gone, and she has
been completely healthy ever since.

Sometimes we doubt how we feel inside and the internal guidance we receive, thinking that we are not "experts." However, we are the expert when it comes to knowing just what should happen in our own life.

Exercises for fostering your child's self-reliance:

- Children are more creative than we give them credit for; when your child is trying to accomplish a task, don't be so quick to swoop in and fix it for him. Give him time to figure it out. You'll be amazed at what he will come up with on his own.

- Let your child "fail." This gives her an opportunity to be responsible for her actions and learn to make a better choice next time.

- Bite your tongue. Observe. Sit back and simply watch your children. Take note of how they figure things out in their own unique way.

- Encourage healthy risk taking. Let your child know that making a mistake is okay—that they shouldn't be afraid of taking a risk. "If you never shoot the ball, you will never make the basket." The most important thing is to try.

four

A conscious mother . . .
teaches her children that they
come from the Divine.

You weren't an accident. You weren't mass-produced. You aren't an assembly-line product. You were deliberately planned, specially gifted, and lovingly positioned on the Earth by the Master Craftsman.

—Max Lucado

When we teach our children that we all come from the Divine,* it is empowering because we understand that we originate from a source greater than ourselves, inheriting godly attributes and potential. We also understand that greatness is not just this wonderful, esoteric, elusive, God-like feature that only the special among us will ever taste. Greatness is something that truly exists in all of us. This is our birthright.

---

* When writing this manuscript, I use the word *God* when describing the source of all that is—the Divine, the I Am that I Am, the Alpha and Omega. Choose the name that works best for you. God has many names, and He answers to them all. I choose to use the word *God,* with a capital G and the pronoun He, for impact, and out of respect.

When we understand this—that we are literally a child of God, endowed with greatness—we tend to behave in such a manner. If a child is told he will be successful, he probably will be successful. If a child is told he will fail, he probably will fail. Henry Ford said, "Whether you think that you can, or that you can't, you are usually right." I agree with Mr. Ford. If we can instill in our children the belief that they are magnificent, powerful, divine beings, chances are they will become magnificent, powerful, divine beings.

One of my spiritual mentors, Deepak Chopra, tells us, "You are a radiant, cherished, and deeply loved being, imbued with the seeds of divinity, and [you] possess the power to live a life filled with love, joy, health and passion, friends, material possessions, and whatever else you choose." There is something of divinity within each of us. We must teach our children to believe with conviction that they have tremendous potential to do good in the world, and that this quality is part of their inherited nature.

To remind my daughters of their inherent value and real identity, I share the following story: During the American Civil War, some soldiers would stencil or scratch identification information into the soft lead backing of their army belt buckles, so that others would know their identity. The military soon instituted the use of dog tags for every person enlisted. I had ID tags made for my daughters to wear with the words *beautiful, brilliant, powerful, radiant, leader.* If they ever feel lost or need a reminder of who they *really* are, they can just read their ID tag, remember, and live fearlessly. Not only have my daughters enjoyed wearing these dog tags, but their friends have also requested them, too. They wear their dog tags with confidence and pride, understanding who they really are. Usually our children are focused on having the latest and greatest technology or fashion fad. We need to remember that instead of only buying our children the latest fashion or high-tech gadget, it's also important to give them meaningful gifts that remind them of how special they are, and that instill them with confidence.

Listening for Answers

Our children should also know that we can commune with God, go within, and receive answers to anything—anytime. No middleman, just you and your Heavenly Partner, whatever that means to you. We should allow our children opportunities to understand this truth.

My youngest daughter Lola had just returned to school after being out for a week due to a flu virus. I picked her up from kindergarten and she skipped to the car, asking if we could stop by the deli to get some homemade chocolate chip cookies. My inclination was to say no and go home for a healthy lunch. Then I thought, *Here's a perfect opportunity to teach this little one to go inward and find the answer for herself.* I explained to Lola that she could find out the answer of just what her body needed; she didn't need to ask me. "Just ask your heart and listen," I said. "You will find the answer there."

I looked in the rearview mirror to see Lola's face beaming with excitement. Her joy was oozing from her smile at being allowed to decide for herself; of course she was going to choose the delicious cookie! Moments passed, and slowly her shoulders slumped and her smile drooped to a frown. She mumbled with disappointment, "A banana. My heart wants me to have a banana." She then continued, "I am never going to ask my heart again." We receive guidance through intuition, inspiration, and synchronicity.

Now, you're probably wondering, *What would you have done if she'd chosen the cookie?* This is where we need to allow our children opportunities to figure out the answer for themselves and reap the benefits or suffer the consequences. In the example of Lola and the chocolate chip cookie, I knew that if she chose the chocolate chip cookie, the worst thing that could happen was that her stomach would be upset and she wouldn't feel so great. After we give our children the opportunity to go within and discover solutions for themselves, we can talk to them and point out the success or failure they may have experienced from the situation. With Lola, we talked about how delicious the cookie would have tasted, and how she probably would have felt sick to her stomach, because she was not giving her body the nutrients it needed. The banana really was the better choice for her. I congratulated her for being so wise, and brave enough to listen to her heart—even though her mind was telling her to get the cookie.

This idea is very similar to the previous chapter on self-reliance and discernment. The key to this chapter is to understand and teach our children the power that lies within each of us, and the fact that we have access to this power and its infinite possibilities all of the time. When we understand that we have a "direct line" to God, we can obtain the perfect answer to any of life's questions at any time.

After my diagnosis of multiple sclerosis, I clearly understood that I am not my physical body. I am so much more than my body. Although I love my body, I appreciate that it is simply a vehicle to get me through this life. If I thought I was only my body, I would be totally depressed, because my physical body is very limited right now. Conversely, when I take time to go within and connect with my inner being, I feel the vastness of my true self.

When I am struggling and need guidance, this is the prayer I say: "Dear Heavenly Father, I trust that You know the solution or answer to every situation and every problem. You do a pretty good job of keeping all of the stars and planets in alignment, so you must know the perfect answer to my problems. Show me and guide me to that answer. Make the answer very clear, so I will have no doubt as to what path I should take." Then I wait.

Amazingly, the answer always appears. This takes practice and deep faith, to know that God will provide a way. A powerful verse in the Bible tells us, "And all things, whatsoever ye shall ask in prayer, believing, ye shall receive" (Matthew 21:22). And this is the magic formula: Ask, believe, and receive. One key point of focus is in the first few words, *and all things*. If your child asks you for a piece of bread, would you give him a stone? No. When we understand that we are the offspring of a deity, we can have full confidence in knowing that if we ask and believe, we will receive. In all things.

I have days when I really struggle. Sometimes I just cry, because simply existing is difficult, breathing is difficult, sitting up is difficult, even lying in bed is uncomfortable and challenging. I see my family growing, having fun, encountering challenges, and moving through life. I want to fully participate with the people I love the most, and I cannot at this time. I want to drive my daughter to school, but my ability to drive a car is limited. I would enjoy finger-painting with my youngest daughter, but I cannot open my fingers to spread the paint on the paper. When I have these moments, I call a close friend or visit with a family member, and they remind me of who I really am. They remind me of the Divine source from which I originated.

As I am writing this chapter about teaching our children they come from the Divine—understanding the power we possess to live a completely abundant and joyful life, and receive any answer we need, anytime—I recognize that I have the opportunity to work at this daily. I do not pretend to have this all figured out. Sometimes I don't get it, but I am practicing every day. I make the choice to live my life from a deeper, wider center—the essence of who I am.

Observing nature we find a beautifully balanced ecosystem. In the winter the trees lose their leaves, birds fly south, and insects become dormant. Every aspect of nature receives exactly what is needed so that every spring, the leaves, birds, and insects return. Ultimately, we must have an understanding that we will receive exactly what is needed, because we originate from that joyous, powerful infinite source.

When we look at the structure of a classic bicycle wheel, we see a few important elements: the rim, the spokes, and the hub. The hub is at the center part of the wheel, and every spoke originates from the hub. The spokes then reach and stretch to the outer rim, working together to connect the rim to the hub. Each one of us is like an individual spoke on the wheel. We all originate from the same Divine source, and we are each stretching to reach our unique place in life.

I especially needed guidance in my life at a time when I was not doing well with my multiple sclerosis. I felt that I needed medical care, and possibly to be placed on a disease-modifying medication. But four months after my diagnosis of multiple sclerosis, I was illegally dropped from my health insurance provider, meaning that I would have to pay for all of my treatments out-of-pocket. I could not afford the care and medication I needed. Feeling frustrated, and not knowing what path I should follow, I uttered the above prayer, having faith that God would guide me to the perfect solution.

Three days later, I received a call from my neurologist, who suggested that I call UC Davis Medical Center. "They are going to begin a research study for a new medication," he said, "and you would be a perfect candidate." I would be able to receive medical attention and medication at no cost to me. *Isn't that interesting,* I thought. *I will be able to receive the care I need without having to pay for it myself.* I was selected to participate in the study for the next three years.

Having Faith in Their Choices

Giving our children the opportunity to build a relationship with God, and to honor their own discernment, will carry them through any of life's challenges. I think we will be pleasantly surprised at how our children will soar. Allowing our children this opportunity builds confidence. They will understand that they can tap into intelligence and harness a power greater than themselves. They will understand that they have been imbued with infinite potential, and that it can't be taken away.

Recently I read a brief but very poignant quote by Guillaume Apollinaire:

"Come to the edge," he said.
They said, "We are afraid."
"Come to the edge," he said.
They came.
He pushed them . . . and they flew.

We all have access to every answer we could possibly need. Give your children the chance to fly by allowing them opportunities to discover for themselves that they can find the perfect solution to any question in their life. I am always pleasantly surprised when I give my children the option to choose for themselves and see how they arrive at the perfect answer.

Sometimes, this is easier said than done. We may feel like we would make a better choice for our children, and maybe that is so. But, if we can guide them and ultimately let them make their own decisions, it will allow them to exercise that "discernment muscle." When our children understand that they have access to receive guidance from the Source they originated from, they will realize how powerful they truly are.

Negativity is not the true nature of a child. With loving attention and care, we can bring out the positive human values in a child. This is true even with rebellious children. A rebellious child may need more attention and encouragement. Help your child know that he is unconditionally loved, and that he belongs. Most children want to be like their parents someday (even if they don't want to admit it). If our children have the knowledge that they come from the Divine, hopefully they will strive to be like the Divine and emulate God-like qualities.

Our Divine Qualities

When we understand the essence of who we are, we begin to show more honor and respect to others—and to ourselves. We begin to live up to the great and magnificent inheritance with which we have been endowed. We enlarge our horizon of understanding, and we remember that we are loved and honored, knowing we have great and important work to do here, and no one else can do it for us.

Let's take a look at some of the divine qualities we possess and what they mean: integrity, brilliance, virtue, love, compassion, strength, individual worth, kindness, and creativity.

Integrity. According to the *Stanford Encyclopedia of Philosophy,* "Integrity is one of the most important and oft-cited of virtue terms. When used as a virtue term, 'integrity' refers to a quality of a person's character." The definition of *integrity* is part of a code of especially moral values and an unimpaired condition—the quality or state of being complete. We all come to Earth in a state of being complete.

Brilliance. Webster's dictionary defines *brilliant* as having or showing great intelligence, talent, and quality; splendid or magnificent. If we understand who we really are, we would understand that we have access to unlimited answers and unlimited possibilities. There is nothing you cannot do when you understand your own brilliance. A spark of the Divine lives within you.

Virtue. A virtue is a positive trait or attribute. The quality of virtue is an important concept in Chinese philosophy; it is linked to personal character, inner strength, integrity, kindness, morality, excellence, goodness, and divine power. Confucius explains as follows: "He who exercises government by means of his virtue may be compared to the north polar star, which keeps its place and all the stars turn towards it."

Love. We all want to love and be loved. It is important that we, and our children, know that we are deeply and unconditionally loved just the way we are. It is easy to love people who love us back; it is much more difficult to love people who not only don't love us, but also don't even like us very much. To develop the quality of unconditional and unselfish love, we look to God, who makes the sun rise on both the evil and the good, and sends the rain to both the just and the unjust.

Compassion. We feel compassion when we come into the presence of another human being with a passionate desire, willingness, and urgency to comfort and help them. When cultivating the seeds of compassion in our children, we nurture them to empathize and seek harmony with others. Quoting the 14th Dalai Lama, "If you want others to be happy, practice compassion. If you want to be happy, practice compassion." Practicing compassion is a special virtue that has the power to change the world.

Strength. Why is strength of character so important? Because it allows us to carry out our wills freely while enabling us to cope with setbacks in a healthy manner. Strength of character gives us the courage to admit our own faults and weaknesses; it also allows us to look at misfortune clearly instead of just complaining about it. It gives us the strength to keep a foothold when the tide turns against us, and to continue to climb upward in the face of obstacles.

Individual worth. In the Western and primarily American private banking business, an individual whose financial assets are in excess of one million dollars is described as a "high net worth individual (HNWI)" for regulatory and investment purposes. In the entire world, every human being has high individual worth (HIW). In the material world, an individual's worth is measured by material and monetary success. The truth is that we are all of infinite worth. Just because you are here, you matter. You are not your past, your mistakes, or your accomplishments. You are more cherished than diamonds, more valuable than precious metals. We have all heard the saying, "You are one in a million." This is a lie! You are not one in a million; you are one in seven billion.

Kindness. Some of the great thinkers of our time, from Martin Luther King Jr. to the Dalai Lama, have had something to say about the importance of kindness. The civil rights leader stated, "Life's most persistent and nagging question is 'What are you doing for others?' " And the peaceful spiritual leader called doing good deeds "our prime purpose." As it turns out, children are hardwired to be kind. "The desire to help is innate," says David Schonfeld, MD, director of developmental and behavioral pediatrics at Cincinnati's Children's Hospital Medical Center. "At first, children like to help others because it helps them get what they want. Next, they do so because they get praise. Finally, they begin to anticipate the needs of others, and it becomes intrinsically rewarding to do nice things for people in their lives." Kids actually want to help and be kind. It is our job as parents to nurture and guide our children to be kind and helpful. When we teach our children kindness at a young age, it becomes a lifelong habit. We should always lead by example.

Creativity. C. S. Lewis expressed, "Human creativity is indeed a god-like trait." The ability for a human being to be creative makes us unique among all other living species. Anthropology tells us that sophisticated works of art first appeared about forty to fifty thousand years ago. No other species of animal, including the apes, are able to produce, interpret, and understand images of art. A successful life requires that we be creative, allowing us to be open to new directions, challenges, opportunities, and solutions. Life is ever changing and evolving, always becoming new. The only constant in life is that life is constantly changing. It is our ability to be creative that helps us to adapt and evolve. As Divine beings, we do not live our lives just by instinct; we have also been endowed with the virtue of creativity. We are able to create our lives through visionary and imaginary thought, enabling us to be driven and reflective upon our lives, giving man the ability to dream and create the future he desires.

Mind is the master power that molds and
  makes,
And Man is Mind, and evermore he takes
This tool of Thought, and, shaping what
  he wills,
Brings forth a thousand joys, a thou-
  sand ills:—
He thinks in secret, and it comes to pass:
Environment is but his looking-glass.

—James Allen

Each of these divine qualities is important to foster in our children, because these qualities are lasting. When we live our lives with these honorable characteristics, we experience profound success.

Exercises for engaging the Divine:

- Practice on your own. Ask God for guidance, and then sit in silence, knowing He will answer. Wait for His reply.

- Now give your child the same opportunity. When approached with a personal question, guide your child to be introspective, to ask God for guidance, and to wait for His response. Understanding this at a young age will help your child lead a confident, powerful life.

- Sit down and make a list of all the wonderful, beautiful Divine qualities that your child possesses. Now share that list with your child and watch how he lights up. Deep down inside, he knows how special he is—but it's always nice to hear it from someone else. He will feel loved when he knows how special he is to you, too.

- Harness your God-given trait of being creative. Knowing that the world reflects back your thoughts, clear your mind, sit for a moment, and create a detailed vision of what you would like the universe to reflect back to you. Remember, "The greatest achievement was at first and for a time a dream. The oak sleeps in the acorn, the bird waits in the egg, and in the highest vision of the soul a waking angel stirs. Dreams are the seedlings of realities." —James Allen

Dream big!

five

A conscious mother . . .
gives her children presence.

*Your hand opens and closes, opens and closes. If it were always
a fist or always stretched open, you would be paralyzed. Your
deepest presence is in every small contracting and expanding,
the two as beautifully balanced and coordinated as birds' wings.*

—RUMI

I have learned that one of the most important things I can give
my children is to be completely present to every moment I am
with them. Sometimes, this feels challenging when there is so
much to accomplish in a day, so many demands for our attention. But this is something any mother can do, regardless of her
challenges. Some of us struggle with financial challenges, relationship challenges, or health challenges. I'm here to tell you
that this can be done even with life-altering health challenges.
Life seems to get busier and busier with every passing day. Even
as you are reading this book right now, what are you thinking
about? Are you really concentrating on these words, or are you
thinking about what you need to do next? Are you thinking, "I
really shouldn't be reading right now; I've got so much to do"?

We are usually multitasking, distracted, and feeling pulled to do something other than what we are doing right now.

When you truly dwell in the present moment, it makes you a person that others want to be with, work with, share ideas with, and share their lives and dreams with; this energy is the spiritual basis for creating close relationships. We want to create this type of close relationship with our child. By being present, you are honoring and respecting your child. You're saying, "You matter more to me than anything else going on in the world right now." This is a great model for your children; also, don't be surprised when they begin extending more honor and respect toward you! I have noticed that when I make the effort to be present when my children are sharing with me, they tend to want to open up and share even more because they feel they are being heard. What a beautiful experience, especially when raising adolescent children, because this type of open sharing can be a rarity.

In the dictionary, the word *present* has many meanings. As a noun, it is a gift; as a verb, it means to become manifest; and as an adjective, it means to be attentive or immediate. Being truly present is a gift for others, and for ourselves. We cannot manifest in the past or the future; we can only manifest in the here and now. This requires a state of being fully present, which means being truly attentive.

Being Present When They Want to Talk
Being present with my young children is very different from being present with my older children. I have found that I

need to be available to visit and listen when my older children want to talk and share their lives, usually between ten and eleven p.m., which is generally my bedtime. When my oldest child, Scott, was a sophomore in college, just about every night he would come into my bathroom just when I was tired, unwinding, and wanting to get right into bed. I knew that what he wanted to share was important to him. So, instead of taking out my contacts, brushing my teeth, and washing my face while he was sharing with me about his life, I would be completely present and listen to every word he had to share. It seemed to be the same conversation every night: "I would like to go to medical school; what do you think about UC Davis? I'm really enjoying my EMT class and learning about the human body . . ." On and on he went, sharing with me what was important to him.

One night, he came into my room and said, "Mom, I'm really glad to have you. You're the only one who will really listen to me when I talk about things I would like to do in my life, like medical school. Everyone else seems to get bored with it." I realized then that even though I was tired and wanting to just get into bed, it was really important to my son that I was available to him. And you know, the more I was present for Scott, the more I really enjoyed our conversations. I began to look forward to our late-night visits and learning about his life and what was important to him.

Research shows that we speak at a rate of about 125 words per minute, yet we have the capacity to hear up to 400 words per minute. So, what are we doing with that extra space in our minds when we are listening to someone speak? Are we really being present and listening? Or are we thinking about something else to fill in the gap? Listening is essential to having a fulfilling relationship with our children—or anyone, for that matter. If you are having a challenging time with one of your children, consider examining your listening skills and whether you are truly present when visiting with your child. There are great benefits to listening well: Your child will feel more drawn to you, you will have opportunities to learn something new about your child, and she will understand that there is no one more important to you in that moment.

Now, rewind eighteen years. . . . When I was a young, new mother, I was fascinated by how quickly my newborn son was growing. Each day brought changes and growth; I wanted to capture every moment. One evening, after giving my son a bath, I sat next to his crib and held him in my arms, rocking him to sleep. I didn't want to ever forget the moment, so I "made" a memory. With all of my senses I took it in. I could feel the warmth of his tiny body, wrapped in a blanket in my arms. I could feel the hypnotic sway as I gently rocked him back and forth. I could smell the sweet scent of baby lotion on his freshly washed little body. The soft sound of lullabies filled the air. Even now, twenty years later, if I close my eyes and recall this memory, it feels like I am experiencing that moment again. Being present to the moment and making a memory help me to remember this special time with my newborn son. Try this with your children. Capture a meaningful moment together so that you will always remember it.

Being present with my younger children may look something like this: Once a week my youngest daughter has a spelling test. She needs help to study, someone to dictate her spelling words to her. I have found that Lola is much more confident and focused on her spelling words if I am completely present to the task at hand. Or, my middle school-age daughter arrives home from school, runs upstairs to my room, and plops on my bed, full of excitement. She explains that only five people passed the history test, and guess what? She was one of the five!

It can be challenging to be fully present when our children need us to be there for them, because they may be interrupting our lives and schedules. I have found there are a couple of things I can do; if it truly is an interruption to something important I am trying to accomplish, I let my child know that I am completely interested in what she has to share, and I will have to get back with her when I can fully pay attention. Then I finish up what I am working on and call the child back when I can fully listen. If it is not something so important, I stop what I am doing and fully listen to my child.

Remember, there are no second takes at living this moment right now.

In his book *The Power of Now,* Eckhart Tolle shares, "Realize deeply that the present moment is all you have. Make the now the primary focus of your life." Thank you for the beautiful reminder, Eckhart. The mind lives in continual memory of the past or in anticipation of an imaginary future. The now is all there is; even the future will be just another "now" when the time comes. Therefore, it is vitally important that we make a conscious choice to be in the present moment with our children. I am sadly reminded of the lyrics to Harry Chapin's song, "Cat's in the Cradle," where a father is not present to his son when his son is young, and sadly, he misses out on his life. When the father is older and finally has time to spend with his son, it's too late, and the son doesn't have time for his father. The only time we have is right now. Enjoy the present moment and make time to be fully with your child.

Beggars are those who do not find truth and joy inside; they may be rich financially yet beggars for emotions. Those who look outside for "scraps" of pleasure, do not realize it lay in their heart.

— *Eckhart Tolle*

Exercises for being more present with your child:

- Take some time to meditate. There are many forms of meditation; find one that works for you. It can be as simple as closing your eyes, taking a deep breath, and simply sitting still for a moment. Developing a daily practice in meditation will quickly hone your skills for being present.

- Next time you have a moment with your child, stop whatever you're doing and listen; really hear what she is saying and experience the moment.

- Using all your senses, make a memory.

- The next time your child wants to visit, stop everything you are doing and really listen. If it is not a good time to fully give your presence, let your child know that you will get back to him soon. Finish what you are working on and invite your child back; then, be present, deeply and fully.

- Pay close attention to your daily routine. For example, when you are washing dishes, really sense the warmth of the water, smell the scent of the dish soap, feel gratitude for the moment. It is through our presence that we feel peace and are thankful for where we are, now. We enter a state of presence through our attentiveness.

six

A conscious mother . . . gives her children opportunity for service.

I don't know what your destiny will be, but one thing I know: the only ones among you who will be really happy are those who have sought and found how to serve.

—ALBERT SCHWEITZER

The greatest service our children can learn is to serve one another. Let me say that one more time: The greatest service our children can learn is to serve one another. We tend to love more deeply that which we serve. For some reason it is not easy or enjoyable for my children to help one another; it seems they would prefer to do a kind deed for a friend.

When our children are actively engaged in giving service, they begin to cultivate a sense of empathy. Empathy takes place when we are able to put ourselves in the shoes of another and really feel their pain, joy, hardships, and happiness. When we have developed the characteristic of empathy, we are able to listen to another and understand what is needed, whether it be spoken or unspoken. The Dalai Lama states, "We need another way to promote human value. . . . We are all part of the same human family." Giving service opens our eyes, helping us to be in touch with our own humanity, and it is another way to promote human value.

James Brabazon, author of the biography of Albert Schweitzer, defined "reverence for life" with the following statement: "Reverence for Life says that the only thing we are really sure of is that we live and want to go on living. This is something that we share with everything else that lives, from elephants to blades of grass—and, of course, every human being. So we are brothers and sisters to all living things, and owe to all of them the same care and respect that we wish for ourselves." When we give service, we are showing care and respect for others.

Service is something that needs to be experienced. By writing the word *honey* on a piece of paper and then licking it, you do not taste its sweetness. So it is with service. You have to experience it to taste the sweetness.

Humankind has approached a critical crossroads—of decency, graciousness, moral fiber, honor, and integrity. Our most upstanding and virtuous inclinations are threatened at every turn. And our families are sensing the tension with considerable intensity. Mary Pipher, author of *The Shelter of Each Other,* shares the same sentiment: "Families in America have been invaded by technology, mocked by the media, isolated by demographic changes, pounded by economic forces, and hurt by corporate values." She concludes that families are "thirsty in the rain." Especially in times of crisis, we turn to our families for safety, caring, and love. One way that we can combat the outside tensions on our family is to mix in kind acts of service for one another. Today family members are often living in the same dwelling but frequently are not interacting or connecting one with another. Service allows opportunities to connect on deeper levels with each other. Service cultivates unity, harmony, and prosperity.

Is it innate within us to serve one another? I would like to think, yes. When we reflect back through time and look at the formation and structure of the family and clan for earlier inhabitants of the Earth, we see instinctive measures of service. The mother gives the ultimate service in giving birth to her young. The baby is completely reliant upon the service of its mother for survival and safety. The mother is reliant upon the father to provide food, shelter, and safety for herself and their young. The father is reliant upon the elder men and younger men to stay with his family while he goes out and hunts for food. There must be a perfect balance of service given by, and to, all of the members of the family for the survival of the family unit or clan.

In our families we experience much of the growth we will obtain in our lifetime; we reside with, serve, teach, and learn from each other. While we cannot choose the exact conditions of our family, we can choose every day to make our families stronger and more joyful. One way of doing this is through service to one another. We recognize that every family member's involvement is important for the success of the family unit. The responsibility of creating a success-ful family is too large for any one person. This is one of the reasons why working together as a family to love and serve one another is essential. In a disaster or crisis situation, I have never heard a victim say, "I need to check my bank account," or, "Let me get to my to-do list." Instead, we always hear a victim voicing concern for the well-being of family members. Let's not wait for a disaster to take place before we serve within our family. We can offer simple acts of service on a daily basis, reassuring our family members that they are valued and deeply loved.

Household Chores Can Be a Form of Service

When disability started to affect my ability to care for my home and family, and I was losing my capacity to walk and use my arms and hands effectively, I needed my children to pitch in and help out more around the house. At first I felt guilty; *I should be taking care of my family*. But I decided to look at this situation differently . . . I was giving my children a gift: an opportunity to learn how to work together as a family and to serve one another. My children have also been given the opportunity to give service to their mother. It is one thing to work hard, but when the hard work is coming from a heart geared toward service, it becomes a deeper, more meaning-ful effort. As I have lost some use of my fingers, my oldest daughter has been given the opportunity to braid her little sister's hair. My son will carry me to my bedroom when my legs are too weak to make it upstairs. When dinner needs to be prepared, my adolescent daughters jump right in to help get the meal on the table for our family. When I am too weak to roll over in bed, my youngest daughter can help to move my body so I am a bit more comfortable. These actions are more than just doing work; these efforts come from a heart of giving service.

Instead of me doing most of the cleaning around the house, my children have to pitch in and help. They have all learned and can appreciate the hard work it takes to make a household run smoothly. Don't get me wrong; they are not always elated to help out. Sometimes they would rather just relax or be on their iPhone/iPod/iPad, texting their friends, but in the end they have a real sense of satisfaction and happiness that only comes from helping others. My husband likes to share with our children what he calls an ancient Chinese secret: "Many hands make light work."

In the summer months, when my children are out of school, I create a chart that lists different tasks they can do to be useful and helpful around our home. This helps them to be productive and keeps them busy for the first part of the day. They no longer need to wake up and ask me all morning, "Mom, what are we going to do today?" Their chart will keep them busy for most of the morning. Depending on their age, this chart might include tasks such as: get dressed, brush your teeth, make your bed and clean your room, vacuum, read for a half-hour, feed the cat, and so on. No matter the age, there is one item that is always on the list: secretly do a good deed for another. My youngest daughter enjoys surprising one of her sisters by making their bed. Lola feels good about herself, and the recipient of her good deed feels appreciated and loved.

Society would have us believe that struggle is a weakness. In reality, we become stronger through struggle. Our family has been given this gift of becoming stronger, due to my physical limitations. The good news is that it doesn't have to take a chronic health challenge to create this opportunity in your family. All you have to do is make time to work together and serve one another.

Giving Service outside the Home

Sometimes giving service to others sounds overwhelming. We can think of simple ways to serve others so that it becomes a part of every day. We should also provide opportunities for our children to serve outside of the home. By teaching our children the importance of giving service, we teach them human value and empathy.

When you give to another person, you are, in essence, admitting that you have an understanding of the grand scheme of human kindness. We are teaching our children to live beyond selfishness, beyond greed, beyond their personal needs. We are living from our higher selves.

According to educator, writer, and speaker Leo Buscaglia, "You want to be the most educated, the most brilliant, the most exciting, the most versatile, the most creative individual in the world, because then you can give it away; and the only reason you have anything, is to give it away." I tell my children, If you ask me for a piece of gum and I don't have gum with me, can I give you a piece of gum? The answer is no. You cannot give of what you do not have. When we take time to cultivate attributes of giving and being self- less, we then have something to share.

One Christmas our family was busy packing up our house to move to a new home. Everything needed to be boxed and ready for the moving company to load two days before Christmas. We would be meeting them at our new home the day after Christmas. Because all of our belongings were com- pletely in boxes, we chose not to celebrate the Christmas hol- iday in our usual way, with Santa Claus and exchanging gifts. We decided to cook and serve food to the homeless at a local shelter. It was by far one of the most unique and special holi- days we'd ever spent together as a family. By giving service to the less fortunate, it helped my family to appreciate all of the many blessings we have in our lives.

It is said that it takes one hundred years for an olive tree to produce good fruit. Once an olive tree reaches the point of producing good fruit, it will produce fruit for generations. It can also take some time before good habits, like serving others, will become a natural part of our children's lives. Just like the olive tree, once we reach the point of producing good habits, it will stick for generations. Make the effort and take the time to nurture these good habits; it will be worth it in the end. Conversely, it only takes an onion plant nine weeks to grow, produce an onion, and die. Let's invest the time to produce olives instead of onions.

It can be a delicate balancing act, understanding how to serve self, family, others, community, and the world. If we are only serving ourselves, then our lives become very egocentric, self-centered, and self-absorbed. At the same time, we must remain aware of our own needs, and make sure those needs are met. If our only attention is on serving our family, we miss out on opportunities to help others, and we may encourage within our children complete reliance on others. This is hazardous, because our children will require that others must always meet their needs rather than realizing they can be self-reliant. Likewise, if all of our energy and attention is directed toward serving others in the community, or the world, we will completely miss out on serving our greatest gift—our family.

Exercises for encouraging service:

- Sit down with your children and explain the importance of family and giving service to one another.

- Take a moment to make a list of household chores. Divide this list among family members, and start working together to accomplish the tasks.

- I once watched a TV show where the mother would assign a child a "jurisdiction." This was empowering for the child, because it was his own area of responsibility. This week, assign each child his or her own "jurisdiction." It may be the dishwasher jurisdiction or the sweeping jurisdiction. See how quickly they take ownership of their little corner of the house.

- Pick one drawer, or one cupboard, for each family member to clean out and organize. Do this every day for one week, and see how quickly your house becomes organized. All the while, you're spending quality time together and creating an environment that fosters teamwork.

- When experiencing struggles, look at your challenges as a gift—an opportunity to lovingly give service to each other and become a stronger family unit.

- Every week, ask yourself, "Where can I serve *with* my children?" Become aware of the needs of those around you, and select something that you and your children can do to serve others. When I think of giving service with my children, I think of feeding the homeless at a local food bank. But serving others can be incorporated into our daily routines. It could be something as simple as baking and delivering cookies to a family with young children, or when out running errands, paying special attention to the people you encounter and greeting them with a friendly smile.

- If you come across military servicemen, be sure to thank them for their service, and encourage your children to do the same.

seven

A conscious mother . . . takes it slow.

Beware the barrenness of a busy life.

—SOCRATES

Somehow, we've created a fascination with busyness—with children involved in multiple sports, music, school, clubs, church, dance, and all sorts of extracurricular activities that leave little or no time for family or self-reflection. The modern idea of family dinner consists of drive-through meals eaten in the backseat of the car while shuffling to the next activity, or eating dinner while zoning out in front of the TV.

Last night, as we were sitting down to have dinner, two family members served themselves first, sat at the table, and began to eat. Two other family members were trying to dish out their meals. The youngest one was having trouble serving herself. It was chaotic and frustrating. I stopped my family and said, "We are going to wait for the meal to be ready, set the table, give thanks and bless the food, and sit down for a few minutes to enjoy a family dinner together." One of my daughters began to whine that most of her friends don't ever eat dinner together with their family. I was dumbfounded as I asked, "What do your friends do for dinner?" She responded that it was left up to them to get their own food.

It seems that life is moving at warp speed. We eat fast, talk fast, walk fast, drive fast, and play fast. We even sleep fast. Most of us judge how busy we are by how much we have to do. When we have a full to-do list, we think we're busy and industrious, and when there isn't much to do, it feels like we're not productive at all. But, in fact, we can feel busy when there isn't much to do, and we can feel relaxed even when there's a lot going on. The states of "busy" and "not busy" aren't defined by what's on your list of things to do. Contrary to what most people think, there is no such thing as multitasking; the brain can tend to only one thing at a time. Being too busy or not being busy is merely an interpretation of our level of activity. Busyness is a state of mind, not a fact. No matter how much or how little we're doing, we're always just doing what we're doing, simply living this one moment of our lives.

Enjoy Dinner Together as a Family

We are really missing out on a very critical time in the day to connect with our children if we do not take a few minutes to sit down, visit, and eat a meal together. I have always felt like there is something off if we are too busy to take fifteen or twenty minutes at dinnertime to be together. Sometimes our families may complain that they have more important things to do than sit down and be together, but I promise you—your family will feel loved and that they matter when you take time to slow down, pause, share your day, and be together.

One of the gifts our family has received from my health challenge is the gift of time. We have had to reduce the number of extracurricular activities we are involved in, granting us more quality time with each other. We have had to slow down. Instead of being constantly on the run, we have more time to cook dinner together; we sit and visit while we eat as a family, and then we work together to clean up the kitchen.

Recently I read an article in *Time* magazine, "The Magic of the Family Meal," by Nancy Gibbs. She explains, "There is something about a shared meal—not some holiday blow-out, not once in a while but regularly, reliably—that anchors a family. Studies show that the more often families eat together, the less likely kids are to smoke, drink, do drugs, get depressed, develop eating disorders and consider suicide, and the more likely they are to do well in school, delay having sex, eat their vegetables, learn big words and know which fork to use." As you can see, those are huge benefits for simply eating dinner together as a family on a regular basis. "If it were just about food, we would squirt it into their mouths with a tube," says Robin Fox, an anthropologist who teaches at Rutgers University in New Jersey, about the mysterious way that family dinner engraves our souls. "A meal is about civilizing children. It's about teaching them to be a member of their culture."

Instead of always rushing to this practice or that performance, we have time to light a fire, sit on the couch and visit, help each other with homework, or read a good book together. There is something to be said about "stopping to smell the roses." Colors become more vibrant, smells become more vivid, tastes become more intense, and sounds are more angelic. When you take it slow, everything is more enjoyable. What a blessing it is to have time to enjoy each other's company.

Have a Family Meeting

Now, contrary to my situation, my oldest sister's family is extremely busy and is still able to be high-functioning. From an outsider's point of view, it seems their family is successful because they are each 100 percent committed to the family, and they are each 100 percent disciplined in doing what it takes to create a successful, happy, loving family. I wanted to get an idea of how a family that is so busy can still experience being connected to one another and have a house that is full of love.

She explained that they can be involved in so many activities because they take time once a week to meet together as a family and review what is planned for the week. This gives the family an opportunity to prioritize what is really important for the whole family unit. When reviewing the week they ask themselves, "How can we make this work so everyone feels supported, and we have time to be together?" If one son has a concert on Wednesday, the rest of the family will be sure that it is on their schedule to be at the event. A couple of things are accomplished: The child feels respected, loved, and supported, and the family has a fun outing where they can be together. Mom may be busy on Monday night, so Dad makes sure he is available to make or get dinner. This also gives the family an opportunity to support one family member that may be really busy that week. This is one way parents can model how to show respect, value, and love for one another. My sister Suzanne is sure to plan some downtime for her family to just be together. When we allow our children to be part of this planning process, our kids feel respected and valued, and they know that their opinion matters regarding what will take place with the family. They understand that their lives are just as important as ours.

When we plan as a family to support one another in our weekly activities, each person will feel valued, validated, and loved. My nephew had an important basketball game he was playing in for the local high school. His entire family attended the game to witness his participation and show him their support. It was an important game—if they won, the team would advance to the state finals. As the clock was ticking down, his team was behind by two points, with just a few seconds left in the game. My nephew was at the half-court line and a teammate passed him the ball. He glanced at the clock—six seconds, five seconds, four seconds; as he dribbled, there was not enough time to get to the basket. With all of his might he shot the ball. It seemed to be moving in slow motion. With only two seconds left in the game, the ball swooshed into the basket. The crowd erupted into cheers. He made the basket, the team was up by one point, and they won the game! No doubt it was the best game of his high school career, and his greatest cheerleaders—his family—were there to revel in the moment with him. Can you imagine how different his experience would have been if his family had not been there, and he'd had to come home and try to explain the excitement of making the game-winning shot?

Here is another example of the importance of planning family schedules together. One mother I know was training for her first half-marathon race. It was a Saturday morning, and this would be her first ten-mile run. She was nervous about the long distance, and had prepared with a great deal of training. One of her children sat down with her and helped map out her ten-mile course. She set out for her first long run. It was painful, and she wondered if she could finish. As she approached the halfway point of five miles, she noticed in the distance one of her daughters standing at the corner, holding a cool drink of water and cheering her on. "Way to go, Mom—keep it up! You can do it! Great job!" Her daughter kept cheering as her mom ran past. This gave the mom a renewed sense of strength to complete the last five miles. Although this mom was busy with her training schedule, she felt the full support of her family because they took the time to look over their schedules and find simple ways to support one another.

When we take the time to sit down, plan, prioritize, and communicate with one another, it naturally provides opportunities to encourage and serve one another. I have come to the conclusion that taking it slow doesn't necessarily mean a smaller to-do list; it's more a state of mind.

Exercises for slowing down as a family:

- Cross one activity off your list this week. Wow! That was easy.

- Plan at least one dinner at home. Cook the meal together, eat together, and clean up together.

- If you have little ones, create a bedtime ritual. This is a special time of day; sending your children off to bed with a kiss and a big hug is priceless. For older ones, leave time to check in with them before going to bed. Don't forget a hug and kiss for them, too.

- Learn to say no. Only say yes to those activities that really affect the success of your family. It is said that sometimes no is the best answer we can give.

- Try a moving meditation. Intentionally bring awareness to the movements of your body. Become aware and conscious of how you are moving, and you will feel refreshed instead of rushed.

- Focus on each breath. This will make life a living meditation. You will naturally slow down.

- Schedule time at the beginning of each week to have a family planning meeting. Review each person's schedule and events for the week, and discuss how everyone can make it work so that each family member feels supported.

eight

A conscious mother . . .
instills in her children that their most important job in life is to be their best selves.

Always be a first-rate version of yourself, instead of a second-rate version of somebody else.

—JUDY GARLAND

Each of my daughters, in some form or another, was experiencing the drama of girls comparing girls. They were either feeling superior, or inferior, as they were "sizing" themselves up against the other girls at school. One of my daughters was feeling sad because she did not have a love interest, and her best friend did. She was feeling a little insecure and competitive with her best friend. Just because one friend may have a boyfriend and is experiencing a new relationship doesn't mean that she has taken all of the love in the world, not leaving any for anyone else. In the physical world this may be true. If I have six slices of pizza, and you take one slice, I have less pizza. But in the spiritual realm, it is the exact opposite. The more you give, the more you will receive. For example, if we give more kindness, we will receive more kindness. There is more than enough for everyone. This applies to many things: love, joy, attention, friends, relationships. . . . When we develop this type of knowing, it can help us feel genuine happiness for another's gains and accomplishments without feeling like it somehow takes away from our own success.

Teach Your Children to Be Themselves

Sometimes children, and especially girls, can focus on what other people have and then feel inadequate and less desirable if they don't have equal or more possessions. I felt concerned as I noticed my daughters feeling insecure, inadequate, and in competition with their peers. They were constantly comparing themselves and their life situation to others.

There is a new phenomenon identified as social media depression. According to a report on social media and children, released in late November 2013 by the American Academy of Pediatrics (AAP), when adolescents spend a lot of time on social media sites it leads to classic symptoms of depression. Viewing a constant stream on Facebook that includes happy, boasting status updates and photos of peers having a great time can make kids feel worse about themselves, the *Chicago Tribune* reports. "It can be more painful than sitting alone in a crowded school cafeteria or other real-life encounters that can make kids feel down, because Facebook provides a skewed view of what's really going on." Gwenn O'Keefe, the report's co-author, tells the *Tribune*, "Online, there's no way to see facial expressions or read body language that provide context." Facebook and other forms of social media can increase and intensify feelings of depression because of constant comparison to others' Facebook pages, routinely highlighting only the "best of" things in a person's life.

I sat down and said to each of my children, "Your only job in life is to be the best *you* possible. There is no one who has ever lived on this Earth, or who will ever live on this Earth, who can be a better you than *you!* So, don't compare yourself to anyone else. Don't try to be someone else. Your job is to be you! No one can do it better. You have been put on this Earth for a special purpose, and no one can accomplish that purpose better than *you.*" As I shared this with my children, I was pleased to notice the joy and excitement at their new-found "job." Abigail exclaimed with a sense of relief, "Wow! That's great! All I have to do is be the best Abigail Jensen? That's easy!"

If you are not being you, who is going to play the part you were created to play? There is no one on Earth who can be a better you than you. We are all familiar with the old adage, "You are one in a million." This is not true. You are not one in a million; you are one in *seven billion!* I hope you can feel the power behind that statement, and understand just how unique and special you are. There are seven billion people on the planet, and not one of those people can be you, better than you. Oprah Winfrey cannot be a better you than you. Bill Gates cannot be a better you than you. The President of the United States cannot be a better you than you.

One minute we are telling our children to be themselves, and the next minute they are receiving a confusing message from their friends, the media, and society that they need to be just like everyone else. In that moment they abandon themselves. Our children may try to be themselves and then find that they are criticized and judged for not conforming. Imagine if the Wright brothers would have listened to all of the people telling them their dream would not work just because no one had ever flown before. The world would have really missed out if they had listened to the naysayers and tried to conform. They would have suppressed their dream. How many times do our children suppress their dreams because they want to fit in, and they're afraid of embarrassment, or being different? Don't let the world miss out on the gifts you have to offer, and teach your children to do the same. Be your fullest expression of you. Express your individuality, and bless everyone around you by expanding the brilliance that only you can offer.

Celebrating What Makes Each of Us Unique
Recently I bought a pair of distressed jeans; the tag read, "These jeans are intentionally flawed to make them unique."

Don't ever feel like you need to hide your uniqueness. In fact, you should do just the opposite—let your special uniqueness shine for the entire world to see. We are all "intentionally flawed" to make us unique. We see the individuality in each of our children. I was always amazed at how each one of my children was born with a unique personality, and it was apparent from the beginning—quiet, silly, intense, precious, sweet. Never hide what makes you special. There is power in living life authentically. We each came into this world with a special purpose to share with others, and no one can fulfill that purpose quite like you! A friend of mine once made a comment in regard to showing up as your authentic self. She said, "Think of all of the prayers that will go unanswered if you do not show up being you, and your purpose for being here goes unfulfilled."

The violin does not play the whole symphony; it plays the beautiful part of the violin. Encourage your child to play his own instrument. No one can do it just like him! "We can only be who we are, and at some point that has to be good enough," spiritual teacher Panache Desai reminds us.

Although all of humankind is part of a whole, that unity does not take away from our uniqueness. No two snowflakes are alike, just as no two people are alike. Our individuality accentuates our interconnectedness. We are each spokes of a wheel, all expanding out into a different part of the circle, but where we originate is the same. Focus on uniqueness rather than being special. *Special* is what individuals seek to be. It comes from a place of wanting to be above another, shine brighter than another, or be better than another. Aspiring to be special stems from a system that is built around separateness. Specialness is from comparisons and not connectedness. When one feels unworthy, the need to be special is more of the driving force, as opposed to uniqueness, where no comparisons are made.

I love summertime because it's a time to slow down, relax, and be a bit lazy. School is out, the sun shines more often, and the days are longer. With warmer weather we spend additional time outside, barbecuing, stargazing, eating watermelon, sipping on lemonade, and swimming. As a kid growing up in Arizona, I spent hours and hours outdoors, swimming in the pool. For those of us with blonde hair, this can be problematic, because chlorine can turn beautiful blonde hair into dreadful green hair. Most of my friends with "green" hair were quite embarrassed, but one of my friends completely embraced it, stating, "I love my green hair. It's nice to have a different color for a change." She was able to enjoy and celebrate what made her unique. Discover the attributes that make your child unique. Don't try to change them; embrace them! Always remember that it's your child's uniqueness that makes him so special.

By Recognizing Our Children's Unique Gifts, We Give Them Confidence to Grow

My dad is an incredible man. One of his greatest gifts is his ability to make others feel extra special. When I was a young girl, and throughout my adult life, he has always reassured me, "Julie, you are so wise and intelligent. I have always known that you could do anything you put your mind to, and do it well. I really think you could be the CEO of a major corporation if you wanted." Because of his affirmation and confidence in me, I have always experienced life knowing that I could accomplish *anything*. The genesis of that confidence simply came from my dad.

My oldest sister shared with me an experience she'd had with our father. She was in high school at the time, and she wanted to apply for a foreign exchange program. When discussing her plans with our dad, his response was profound and very empowering. "Of course you should," he said, quickly adding, "They would be crazy not to choose you." This gave Suzanne, at age sixteen, all the confidence she needed to undergo the interview process and eventually be selected as one of four students to represent the United States of America in a foreign country.

Sometimes we don't notice how exceptional we really are. We are like a goldfish swimming in the fishbowl; we swim in the water but don't really notice it. The water is always there whether the fish notices it or not. And so it is with our unique gifts and qualities—those gifts are always there, and sometimes we just don't realize it.

We consider Abraham Lincoln to be one of the greatest presidents of the United States of America. But did you know that Abraham Lincoln overcame great setbacks and obstacles before becoming president in 1860? He had two business ventures fail, lost eight different elections, and had a complete nervous breakdown. It was his self-confidence, courage, and desire to be his best self that kept him moving toward his dream.

Our children will experience disappointments and setbacks in their life's journey, but if we can instill in them the belief that they are unique and special, they will continue on to greatness with confidence. Michael Jordan was cut from his high school basketball team. Beethoven's music teacher told him he was a hopeless composer. Colonel Sanders (creator of Kentucky Fried Chicken) was told "no" by over a thousand restaurants for more than a year while he lived in his car, trying to sell his chicken recipe. More than a hundred banks turned down Walt Disney when he tried to get funding to develop Disneyland. These are all examples of people who knew their greatness and how unique their contributions to the world would be, and did not let others' opinions deter them from accomplishing their dreams.

As parents, we have a tendency to tell our children exactly what they should know or do, without giving them an opportunity to figure this out on their own. Our children can know what they are called to do in life, their purpose, or what they are capable of, and age has nothing to do with one's ability to make this discovery. Our children have, as we do, the same direct link to the source that knows all. Guide your children to come to this unique realization. Even if no one else sees or understands their greatness, our children should know this simple truth: They are irreplaceable.

Guide your children to discover and rise up to meet their life's purpose. Help them understand who they are. They literally are children of God, and they can change the world. Teach them to never underestimate the power they have. It is especially fun to watch our young children discover what they are capable of. We can underestimate our children in so many ways, especially their ability to discover for themselves the purpose for why they are here.

When I was a young girl, my grandfather would take me fishing. Sometimes we would fish while slowly walking a creek; other times he would take me in his boat to go fishing in a lake. My grandpa seemed to know all of the tricks for catching the best fish. I would look up at my grandpa and admire him as he taught me how to bait my hook and add weights, or, occasionally, a bobber, to the line. We would make a careful selection of corn, salmon eggs, or worms; the rainbow trout in the streams seemed to prefer Velveeta cheese. Sometimes the selection for bait was an artificial lure. I would open his tackle box and look at his collection of lures. Some were plain, and some were sparkly with lots of color, made of plastic, rubber, feathers, or shiny metal. "Julie, be careful," my grandpa would say. "Those lures have hooks hidden in them. I don't want you to stick yourself." I listened to my grandpa and was careful picking up and admiring each of the artificial lures. My favorites were the spinners.

An artificial fishing lure is an object attached to the end of a fishing line, which is designed to resemble and move like a fish's prey. The purpose of the lure is to use movement, vibration, and color to catch the fish's attention so it will bite the hook. It is easy for our children to be distracted by the "artificial lures" in life, which can make them feel unimportant, and just not good enough. This is a trap. Some artificial lures for our children include reality TV, and thinking they must behave just like the people portrayed in the show. Other artificial lures could be sports icons with a negative reputation, rappers, or any other entertainer who behaves badly. Our children think it is normal, and that they need to behave just like the celebrities they idolize. An artificial lure may be the latest fashion trend, bling, owning the latest new toy, or the ideal of what is "cool" and having to be with the "in" crowd.

Help your children to understand the magnificence of who they are, so they won't be enticed by various lures, allowing themselves to be hooked by things that are artificial and really do not matter. When they know of their unique splendor, completely, they will make choices with confidence, living their lives fully and being their best selves.

Exercises for helping your child to be his or her best self:

- Take a moment and explain to your children that their only job in life is to be their best possible selves—by far, the easiest job in the world.

- Make it very clear to your child: You are not one in a million; you are one in seven billion. No one can accomplish your purpose for being here on Earth as well as you can.

- Acknowledge your child when you notice her being her authentic self.

- When our children's confidence and self-esteem are lacking, they can lean on your confidence in them. Be sure to celebrate with your child the many reasons why he is unique and special. Chances are, if his mother believes in him, then he will believe in himself, too.

- Notice someone else's accomplishments and develop and hold genuine feelings of happiness for that person.

- Find one quality or trait that is unique to your child. Compliment and praise your child's uniqueness, and encourage her to develop that quality.

nine

A conscious mother . . .
teaches her children to be radiant.

There is no cosmetic for beauty like radiance.

—ANONYMOUS

We live in a culture that still perpetuates the idea that the source of one's value is directly associated with one's attractiveness or level of success. Most people believe that their beauty defines them. If this is our focus, then we will always wind up feeling frustrated and disappointed. You see, there is a hierarchy when it comes to beauty. "She's more beautiful than me," or "I am prettier than her." Society defines what is beautiful, and this changes according to different races, cultures, time periods—even within different communities. If the focus is on being beautiful, eventually you will fall short; most likely, you'll be exhausted because you will run into someone more beautiful, thinner, wealthier, younger, and so on.

This has been especially prevalent with my teenage daughters, as our culture is so heavily influenced by technology: Facebook, Instagram, text messaging, Snapchat, or searching Google, YouTube, and Twitter, to name a few. Their lives have become completely consumed with technology. It's how they communicate with their friends. On the one hand, it's nice that they can stay in touch with their friends. On the other hand, this technology is intrusive. We can be having a conversation, having dinner, or just relaxing, and their phones are constantly lighting up with a new type of message, leaving them with a sense of urgency to respond now.

The most disturbing aspect of this technology is that some of our young kids measure their own value by how many "likes" they receive from a particular photo or post. To make things even worse, the pictures that are posted are not a true representation of their lives. Multiple photos are taken, the best picture selected, and then the photos are manipulated, airbrushed, and distorted so that the picture posted is a "perfect" representation of themselves. It is not real!

My children were on spring break, and I asked one of my daughters what her friends were doing to keep busy during their vacation from school. She replied that a couple of her friends were getting dressed up to go to the park and do a photo shoot. The intention for the photo shoot was to take a picture, post it online for all of their friends to view, and then see how many "likes" they would receive. They are not just looking for the number of "likes" they receive, but also how quickly they receive these "likes."

Everything in the media pushes us to look a certain way, making us all the same. One year the fashion industry promotes flat shoes, and the next year, it will encourage everyone to wear high heels. One year black is in; the next year, gray is the "new black." Now we feel the need to duplicate everything we already have in black, in gray. Next season, it will be back to black again. These trends have nothing to do with fashion; they have everything to do with buying and spending more money. I am not trying to say it is bad or undesirable to be current with the latest fashion craze; I am saying (very loudly) that it should never define who we are, or our value.

Cultivating Radiance instead of Beauty

Finding your beauty isn't about looking exactly like everyone else. It's about accepting oneself—the parts you love and the parts you don't—and then working with all of it. Nick Vujicic is a gentleman who was born with no legs and no arms. Can you imagine? I was uplifted listening to him speak about his approach to life. He said, "You can either be angry for what you don't have, or thankful for what you do have. Do your best, and God will do the rest." Coming from a man who lives his life with no arms and no legs, this is quite inspiring.

We should be teaching the concept of radiance not only to our daughters but also to our sons. TV, movies, and media heavily influence how our children perceive beauty. The entertainment industry tends to objectify women, making it seem that a woman's value is directly linked to her beauty and sexuality. When our children understand that real beauty lies in a radiant person, they will want to develop their inner qualities of radiance.

When our focus is on being beautiful, it can foster feelings of low self-esteem, because there always seems to be someone more beautiful. Cultivating qualities of radiance will encourage a healthy, positive sense of self. Instead of focusing on beauty, teach your children to be radiant. When we focus on being radiant, we start to see the real source of our value and power. Radiance is magnetic. We have all experienced the person who walks in and lights up the room. Not only are people drawn to her, but opportunities also tend to come her way. She seems to have everything she needs in life. This person is confident in who she is, because she has chosen to be authentic, and has taken the time to focus on developing qualities that define who she really is, such as kindness, courage, unconditional love, gratitude for all that she has, strength, and brilliance. Cultivating these traits helps to foster a strong sense of self, developing the fullest and greatest expression of oneself—who you really are.

When we focus on being radiant, we start to see the real source of our value and power. Can you imagine a world where beauty is a source of confidence, not anxiety? When attributes of radiance are developed, we transform into confident beauty. One becomes more radiant when she chooses to be authentic and develop those qualities that define who she really is—strong, loving, kind, resilient, compassionate.

Radiance requires one to be present, showing up and living life from the inside out.

One muggy August afternoon, two little girls, ages four and seven, were running and romping and stomping through the house, and their mother wanted them to settle down. She said, "Girls, we are going to play a quiet game," and this is what she did. She went into the kitchen, boiled eggs, and gave each child one egg and some paints. She said, "We are going to paint faces on our eggs, and when we get through making our egg dolls, we are going to have a play, and at the end we are going to eat our characters." So, she put her little girls on the floor. The four-year-old finished painting the face on her egg in just two minutes. She wanted another egg.

A neighbor had come to the front door, and while the mother was visiting with the neighbor, her daughter approached her, asking for another egg. The mother said, "You will have to wait just a minute." Well, you know what that means to a four-year-old? Nothing. The child went to the kitchen, got a stool, and pulled it up to the stove. The pot of boiling water was on the back of the stove. When she brought the pot forward and put her hand in it to retrieve another egg, of course it burned her. She fell off the stool and brought the pot of boiling water with her. The child was burned from her neck to her knees, covering two-thirds of her body.

She spent several months in the hospital with many complications; her teeth rotted and they all fell out. Every week the doctors came with a razor and shaved her head because of the danger of infection. But she lived. And that was a miracle.

When it came time for the child to go home from the hospital, her parents were so delighted their little girl had lived through the ordeal, they didn't prepare her for what she looked like. Her first outing was to go to Sunday school. She got dressed and all ready to go to church, but when they arrived, some of the other children cried and ran away, and no one would play with her. When the mother came to pick up her child, she realized that although the burns had healed, her daughter's scars went a lot deeper than the ones you could see.

She took her little girl home, put her on the bed, and told her, "You know that what is beautiful about you is on the inside." The mother told her daughter the same words every single day. She never missed a day.

When the little girl started first grade, she didn't look any better; she still didn't have any teeth, and her scars were prominent. Some parents called the school and said, "My child can't learn if he has to sit beside that burned girl." The mom kept saying, "Honey, you really are beautiful. You've got to look inside." By the time she was eight years old, she had her teeth and her scars were beginning to fade. It looked as if her life was going to be normal. But, when she turned nine she had another major setback. The doctors told her she had bone cancer. It was back to the hospital, this time for chemotherapy. It saved her life, but she lost her hair. From the time she was four until she was fourteen, there were no pictures of this child, except for the one this mother put in her little girl's mind: "Honey, you really are beautiful. Come on; look inside."

What a legacy to give a child. This mother helped her child to understand that her beauty came from within. She helped her daughter understand the importance of developing qualities of radiance. This little girl knew she was beautiful because her mother told her so.

Help Your Child Develop Qualities of Radiance

The following is a list of some of the radiant qualities we can inspire in our children:

Courage. The definition of *courageous* is "one that is not deterred by danger or pain; brave." I would also like to add to that definition, "one that is not deterred by *peer pressure,* danger, or pain; brave." When we develop the quality of being courageous, not much can deter our actions and behavior. So many times our children are swayed by peer pressure to make choices that are not necessarily the best for them. Developing courage is a quality that will carry them through many difficult times in their lives. It is also a good idea to make the choice before the situation arises. For example, I have taught my children that it is not a good idea to participate in using drugs. They made the choice when they were young that they would not do drugs. When approached at school, a party, or anywhere else to participate in using drugs, the decision has already been made, making it just that much easier to have the courage to say "no" in the moment. Of course, most parents discourage their children from drug use, and it doesn't always work. But, hopefully, engaging in a real discussion ahead of time, allowing them to ask questions, and giving them the opportunity to make the decision for themselves before they are even in the situation will strengthen their resolve when tested.

Love. I think everyone in life wants to love and be loved. When one develops the attribute of love, that energy can be felt when the person walks into the room. Recently I was privileged to travel to Italy for a peace summit. I traveled with a caregiver to help me get around. A gentleman in attendance observed my friend pushing me around in my wheelchair and helping me with the things I could not do for myself. He asked her, "Who is the woman you are helping? Is she your sister?" My friend replied, "No, she is just a friend." He was surprised to find out I was not her sister, just a friend, as he observed that the care she gave to me was given with great love. He was drawn to and interested in getting to know us simply because of the love he felt in our presence. Love is the most magnetic and attractive quality of being a radiant person.

Compassion and empathy. When we develop the quality of compassion, by nature it will foster empathy. Compassion is defined as sympathetic concern for the misfortunes and sufferings of others. Empathy is defined as the ability to understand and share the feelings of another. When we learn to feel compassion and empathy, it helps us to understand

and feel the value inherent in every human being, and ourselves. The modern world today is filled with self-absorption, narcissism, and lack of caring for others. When the qualities of compassion and empathy are developed, we awaken within ourselves a sense of authentic caring.

Confidence. I have had many people comment on my ability to live my life with confidence. Although I have become disabled and most of my life is spent in a wheelchair, I have chosen to keep my head up and shoulders back with confidence, knowing that I have a purpose here on Earth that is greater than my health challenge, and having faith that God will provide a way. It would be very easy for me to feel sorry for myself and insecure about my life situation. It is a choice I make every day to show up and live my life with confidence and authenticity. Having this kind of confidence is magnetic and attractive, and it has nothing to do with outward beauty.

Gratitude. Gratitude is the quality of being thankful, readiness to show appreciation for and to return kindness. A great practice for cultivating gratitude is to write down a few things we are grateful for every day. By doing this, we tend to move through our day looking for things to be grateful for; we also tend to appreciate the little things in life. People who are truly grateful tend to be radiant and positive.

Kindness. According to the Australian Kindness Movement, we know that "children do not have to be trained to be kind. Kindness can be observed in action in children from a very early age. A baby, hearing another cry, will often join in.

From what researchers can establish, this response appears not to be from a reaction of distress, but rather as an expression of sympathy for the other baby. Researchers hypothesize that the 'sing along' is to let the other baby know they have company and support." Our job as mothers is to create a home environment of kindness so that our children will continue to remember what they came here already knowing—how to be kind. Children learn the value of and practice kindness at home first, before they have friends and schoolmates. When I was a young girl, my mother taught me, "It is nice to be important, but it is more important to be nice." People who express true kindness are attractive to be around.

Generosity of spirit. When a generous spirit is cultivated, it helps us to become aware of another's needs. This is uncommon in young children, yet important to develop. Most children are selfish by nature. They tend to think that the universe revolves around them. We can help our children to learn otherwise as we embody and demonstrate generosity ourselves. Our grade school–age children take their best cues from us. When our children consistently see us being generous, they will want to copy our behavior. It doesn't always have to be a huge act of generosity; it can be a simple wave to say hello or a smile as we walk past a friend. Help your child to be aware of the wants and needs of others.

Grace. The origin of the word *grace* comes from the Latin word *gratas,* meaning "pleasing and thankful; related to grateful." Developing the quality of grace gives rise to a simple elegance and refinement within our children's character. There are many reasons why we would want our children to be gracious people. Most important, it equips them to treat others with kindness and consideration, even when it is not reciprocated. To cultivate a gracious heart, we need to help our children learn to think and react toward others in a kind way. We can help our children understand why graciousness is important. For example, we don't talk with our mouth full of food because it might be unappetizing for others at the table. It's all about learning to think through how our choices may affect the people around us.

Exercises for building radiance:

- Focus on developing qualities that build character. These qualities have nothing to do with being in front of the mirror.

- Don't wear any makeup for a day. Freedom! With confidence, feel how nice it is to just be your radiant, beautiful self.

- Make a choice right now! Talk with your child and come up with a scenario that may happen. Decide now how you would handle that particular situation. Now when confronted with peer pressure, the choice has already been made, making it easier to have courage.

- Point out kind acts; when you see someone doing something kind, point it out to your children. Whether it is a kind deed your child may do or the kind act of another person, point it out. This will build a "library" in your child's mind of things she can do to show kindness to others. Point out her feelings, also. Being kind feels good, and we all want to feel good.

ten

A conscious mother . . . lights up.

Let others see their own greatness when looking in your eyes.
—MOLLIE MARTI

Do you light up when your children walk into the room? It doesn't take much for this to happen. You don't have to purchase anything. You don't have to go anywhere. You don't have to make anything. Just feel the love and excitement of having your child here with you, now.

Look into your child's eyes and realize that you are looking at the most precious creation in the world. You will feel deep love and reverence for the unique gift sitting right before you. Your child will feel that, too.

When challenges arise, and your child feels lost, you can again look into his eyes and with reassurance say, "You may feel lost and you may not know who you are, but *I know who you really are.*" This may seem difficult with a child who knows how to push your buttons. It is said that being a mother is the most difficult job on Earth; no wonder many of us feel exhausted and unappreciated, making it easy to be impatient and distracted.

Most children go through a phase where they do not want to be different than their peers. As e. e. cummings so astutely recognized, "It takes courage to grow up and become who you really are." When our children choose the approval of others over being their true selves, they will most certainly be left feeling empty. Every time we make a small decision to fit in over being authentic, whether as a child or as an adult, we abandon and deny who we are. This is serious business because we risk becoming confused about who we really are. A smart statement that can be a barometer of whether or not we will do something is, "If it doesn't feel good for *me*, don't do it." Help your children learn how to reflect on this for themselves.

Just keep focused on the truth of who this child is, remembering all of the one-of-a-kind gifts, talents, and qualities he possesses. He will feel how uniquely special he is by seeing your face light up when he enters the room. We live wholeheartedly when we live from a sense of worthiness. When you light up when your child walks in the room, he immediately senses that he is worthy, simply because your radiant face speaks of how your heart feels.

It is well known that good communication skills are the foundation for any successful relationship. It is important to be aware that it is our nonverbal communication—our facial expressions, gestures, eye contact, posture, and tone of voice—that speaks the loudest. Nonverbal communication is a powerful tool in expressing how we truly feel. When your child walks into the room, you may say that everything is fine, but your facial expression says otherwise. Your child will feel appreciated and loved when he sees your face light up.

The eyes are frequently referred to as the "windows to the soul," since they are capable of expressing a great deal about what a person is feeling or thinking. And facial expressions are among the most universal forms of body language. The expressions used to convey happiness, fear, sadness, anger, and excitement are similar throughout the world. Pay close attention and be keenly aware of what you are communicating to your children through your facial expressions. Light up when you see your child.

If we take a look at a growing sunflower, the flower's face follows the sun throughout the day. The head of the sunflower faces east in the morning, and by the end of the day it faces west. The flower is attracted to the light and warmth. This is a beautiful analogy: When we light up in the presence of our children, they too will be attracted to our warmth and light.

Keep Your Critical Face in Check

The common denominator in every human experience is that each person wants to be appreciated and validated. Years ago, in an interview with Oprah Winfrey, best-selling author Toni Morrison shared her wisdom: "It's interesting to see when a kid walks in the room, your child or anybody else's child; *Does your face light up?* That is what they are looking for." She continued, "When my children used to walk in a room, when they were little, I looked at them to see if they had buckled their trousers, or if their hair was combed, or if their socks were up. And so, you think your affection and your deep love is on display because you are caring for them. It is not. When they see you, they see the critical face. They ask themselves, *What's wrong with me now?* I tried from then on to let my face speak what is in my heart, because when they walk in the room, I was glad to see them." It is just as small as that. Oprah then responded to Toni, "That is what I think is so profound, because that is how you learn what your value is. Not by what the person is saying to you, but by what you feel."

Even now, as an adult woman and mother with five children, I can call my own mother and feel her love and excitement just because I called. She is always available to chat. We can talk about what I am making for dinner, something that is challenging for me, or a new decorating idea. The topic of conversation doesn't matter; she is thrilled, and wants to hear every detail. It is reassuring to have someone who is reliably happy that I exist. I have learned from her example; even though I might be busy when my children enter the room, I pause and make sure that they know by the look on my face that I am glad to see them.

When we are critical, whether through our comments or the way we look at our children, it has a negative effect on their sense of self. An overly critical mother probably has her child's best interest at heart, but constant criticism can cause some serious damage to a child's mental health, as well as his relationship with his mother. The criticism can be in the form of a comment or a condemning look. An overly critical mother is the one who is never satisfied—and she doesn't keep her feelings to herself, either. Most of the attention an overly critical mother gives her child is negative. When a child, even as young as a toddler, feels like he cannot do anything right, he'll start to believe there is something wrong with him. When your child walks in the room, put a smile on your face and give him a compliment. Tell him you are proud of him for getting dressed by himself or compliment him on his beautiful coloring, even if it is outside of the lines. Let go of your need for everything to be perfect, and revel in the realization that your child is perfect just the way he is.

Awaken the Possibility in Your Children

We can inspire our children and provide a sense of security by setting boundaries while still allowing them to discover, learn, and be independent. Put your critical face away and give your child some power over his own life. Lovingly show him how to do things by himself. When he can look to you for guidance rather than criticism, he will be more secure and happy.

My father-in-law was a conductor of orchestras, operas, and symphonies. He was a genius, quite a talented man, conducting the most popular and famous symphonies and operas of his time. I have listened to his music and thought his work was beautiful and quite miraculous. You know, a conductor does not make a sound, but to make beautiful music, he depends on his ability to inspire other people and make them powerful, thus creating an exquisite melody for all to enjoy. His job, really, was to awaken possibility in other people.

Our job as mothers is to awaken possibility in our children. How do we know if we are inspiring our children to be magnificent? Look into their eyes. Are their eyes shining? If their eyes are shining, you know you are doing it. If their eyes do not light up, ask yourself, "Who am I being that my child's eyes are not lit up?" This creates a totally different world. American composer Benjamin Zander knows how to inspire and awaken possibility through his brilliant music. He explains this best: "I have a definition of success. It is not about wealth or power; it's about how many shining eyes I have around me." So we can ask ourselves two questions: Do we light up when we see our children? And, do our children's eyes shine when they are in our presence?

Exercises for lighting up in your child's presence:

- This week, make it a point to only focus on the good, positive qualities in your child. This will create a positive snowball effect. The more you see, the more you will get, and the more you will notice special qualities. See how this works?

- Take a moment and look into your child's eyes. Connect with the essence of who she is. And remember the saying "God don't make no junk!"

- Praise the positive qualities of your children.

- Check in with yourself and ask, "Who am I being in this moment?" Be sure that you are a person that others will enjoy being around.

- When your child walks in the room, put a big smile on your face and give him a genuine, heartfelt compliment. Tell him, "I am proud of you . . ." and fill in the blank. He will start to see his worth, and his self-esteem will soar.

- Our children rarely remember what we have taught them, but they always remember how we made them feel. Start noticing what you enjoy about your child, and go out of your way to acknowledge and compliment your child's excellence.

eleven

A conscious mother . . . is a container.

There is nothing more important than a good, safe, secure home.
—Rosalynn Carter

When your child is struggling, you can be a container by embracing her pain, fear, and grief. As mothers, we tend to "over-care" sometimes. Think about it like this: When a passenger on a boat has fallen overboard, the crew does not dive into the ocean to bring him back in. The crew will toss him a lifeline and reel him in to safety. The same applies to your child: Don't try to fix it. Toss her a lifeline, and let her know that you are there for her, as a witness, and to stand with her as she figures out her life. You will be a container to help hold whatever burden is too heavy for her to carry alone. She will feel a sense of relief, knowing she can take a break from holding in her emotions. You will stand with her in complete love, supporting her as she learns how to move through life. Express to your child, "Instead of taking away your pain, I will sit with you." Create and hold a safe place, and teach your child to feel; now *that* is creating a container.

A friend of mine is a very good, successful, and well-intentioned mother who struggles with the choices her oldest child makes for himself. One evening her son asked her if she could give him a ride to the gas station so he could pick up a pack of cigarettes. She shared with him her concerns about smoking and the ill effects it has on your health. She also told him that she would not give him a ride to get cigarettes. Agitated and frustrated, he replied, "Well, Mom, would you give me a ride if I told you I just wanted to pick up a soda? Do you want me to lie or tell you the truth?" She explained to her son that she always wants him to feel safe in telling the truth, but that does not always mean he will get his way. This was a challenging conversation for both my friend and her son. A couple of things were accomplished: She was able to stay true to her beliefs and parenting style, and she was able to create a safe container for her son to be honest with her about his life. Sometimes we may feel like the statement on a T-shirt one of my friends purchased; it read MOTHERHOOD: THE SHORTEST AND STEEPEST PATH TO ENLIGHTENMENT.

Here is a little history trivia about the Tupperware container. In 1945 Earl Tupper developed a container with a lid that would create an airtight seal to hold, store, and preserve food, making it last longer in the refrigerator. This vacuum seal would extend the life of whatever food was placed in the container. As mothers, we can also create a container or a safe place for our children to share and express their feelings. This is important for our children, so they will know they can turn to us for anything, and they will be secure. If we can offer this space for them when they are struggling and trying to figure out their lives, they will have confidence in knowing it is safe to share with us almost everything happening in their world.

Help Your Child Feel Secure in Expressing Emotions

My oldest daughter McKenna came to me feeling deep sadness. She felt that her closest friendships were dwindling. She had an opportunity to share her feelings with me, and I listened. After explaining how sad she was, she said, "But it's okay; I'm still happy." I wonder where she learned that? As a youngster, my interpretation of how to go through life was that I should always be happy—even at the expense of not validating my own feelings. My response to just about everything in life was to put a smile on my face and be happy . . . water off a duck's back. By living my life in this manner, I became a master at suppressing how I truly felt. I was completely out of touch with my own feelings, virtually invisible to myself.

I wanted McKenna to experience life differently. I stopped her right then and encouraged her to allow herself to feel the sadness and acknowledge her emotions; it was okay to feel sadness and anger for the shifting dynamics of her close friendships. I was there to stand with her and hold her up, to be a witness and safe place for her to experience and express her emotions, to be her container. Feeling relieved and knowing it was okay to explore her emotions, McKenna instantly began to cry. She felt my love for her, and she felt protected. It also provided her the experience of opening up to a wider perspective. By acknowledging her feelings, she was able to validate her emotions and move through her sadness, ultimately experiencing the peace that was waiting on the other side.

Some people feel they need to share everything about their children's lives—the good, the bad, and the ugly. When a child knows that her mother will inform others of anything and everything that she shares with her, it will generate feelings of distrust and low self-esteem instead of a sense of confidence. Be conscious of what you share with others about your child and how she would feel about it.

As you provide a safe container, your child will feel your unconditional love, because you are there for her without judgment. Showing up for your child to be a witness for her life is a powerful, intimate, and sacred experience. The definition of a witness is an individual who, being present, personally sees or perceives a thing; a beholder, spectator, or eyewitness—meaning, "I see you." African languages carry a beautiful depth of meaning. The Zulu greeting *Sawubona* means "I see you," and the response *Ngikhona* means "I am here." Dwelling in the Zulu greeting and in the grateful reply is the implication that until you saw me, I didn't exist. By acknowledging me, you brought me into existence. A Zulu folk saying clarifies this; translated, *Umuntu ngumuntu naga-bantu* means "A person is a person because of other people." By witnessing your children, you become profoundly present, able to stand with—and for—them. You become a container of love. I can't think of a more loving, intimate gesture than being a witness for another's life.

Creating a safe and caring home environment will help to support the social and emotional development of our children. First and foremost, children need to feel safe. There is a hierarchy of "feeling safe." First, our children must feel safe physically—safe from physical threat or injury. Second, our children must feel safe emotionally—safe from verbal abuse, teasing, bullying, and/or threats. Emotional safety refers to an internal sense of being safe.

A young mother was at the park with her shy three-year-old son. He was sitting in the sandbox, playing quietly by himself. A group of young children came over to the sandbox to play with him. When he extended a shovel to share with one of the children, the new playmate kicked over the sand castle he had been working so carefully to build. The little three-year-old boy ran over to his mother, wailing, "Oh no! I want to go home!" Hoping to ease his pain, his mother quickly responded, "You're okay, honey, you're okay. Let me help you build your castle again." But the three-year-old could not be consoled and continued to cry, so the mother took her young son home.

Not wanting her son to feel pain, this new mother made a common parenting mistake. She brushed her son's feelings aside, telling him he was okay. He was not okay; he was upset. His sand castle was ruined. We all need someone to listen to us, especially when we are upset. It never feels good to have someone minimize our feelings or try to convince us that we shouldn't feel the way we do. By providing a safe container for our children to express just the way they feel, we are creating emotional safety, laying the foundation for future social, emotional, and academic success.

Exercises for being a container for your child:

- When your child approaches you with a problem, simply listen, reassuring your child that you are there for her. Work hard to understand what she needs, even when her needs seem unreasonable. Empower her to solve her own problems.

- Consistently be there for your children; when a problem cannot be resolved right away, allow your child to just sit with his emotions and feel what he feels.

- Extend feelings of caring, compassion, and unconditional love to your child.

- Witness and behold your child's life. Be present to your child and really "see" her.

- Set appropriate limits, even when those limits cause frustration and tears.

twelve

A conscious mother . . . is introspective.

We search for happiness everywhere, but we are like Tolstoy's fabled beggar who spent his life sitting on a pot of gold, under him the whole time. Your treasure—your perfection—is within you already. But to claim it, you must leave the busy commotion of the mind and abandon the desires of the ego and enter into the silence of the heart.

—ELIZABETH GILBERT, *EAT, PRAY, LOVE*

I have found that I am my better self when I have taken time daily to pray, meditate, and be introspective. There is a force greater than us all, surrounding us always. And I believe that this force will support us daily, providing just what we need, when we need it. Until I really understood this truth, I lived in fear, not knowing who would take care of me and my family if I were no longer able to do so. I have developed a deep faith, knowing that my family and I will be blessed with everything we need. I remind myself that I have continually called upon an unfailing strength, greater than my own. Taking time to develop a spiritual relationship is vital to our success as mothers. It's kind of like working out, in a way. It takes practice and time to achieve success in losing weight and being fit. Working out can be painful and feel uncomfortable, but the more we practice, the easier it becomes. And no one can do our push-ups for us. So, too, is developing an awareness of inspiration. We have to practice quieting our minds and going within so we can hear the messages given to us. If we are constantly surrounded by noise, always moving and on the go, it is difficult to be receptive.

Recently, I was invited to attend a Global Peace Summit in Italy. Governmental, religious, and spiritual leaders from around the world gathered for ten days to discuss how we can create, promote, and support greater levels of world peace. I had the privilege of meeting and working with Dr. A. T. Ariyaratne (I affectionately call him Dr. Ari). Dr. Ari is the spiritual leader for his country, Sri Lanka, and is lovingly referred to as a modern-day Gandhi. During the conference, Dr. Ari approached me and asked if I meditated. When I responded with a yes, he asked what type of meditation I practiced. I let him know that I just kind of make it up as I go. He invited me to meditate with him. We were attending a press conference at the Piazza del Campidoglio (the Capitol Hill of Rome), and he ushered me to a balcony overlooking the ruins of Rome so that we could meditate together. I will share with you the basic technique of meditation he taught me. First, clear your mind. Second, breathe through your nose. Third, focus on your breath entering and exiting your nostrils. Practice this for five to ten minutes. If a random thought enters your mind, tell the thought to go away because you are meditating right now. Dr. Ari taught me that your mind is more powerful than anything.

I did not know this at the time, but later I learned that Dr. Ari has gathered millions of people to meditate together, addressing the many conflicts in his country. In the same character as Martin Luther King Jr., he has led peace marches and meditations with millions of people. In the likeness of Mahatma Gandhi, he has quieted angry masses through his personal example. Just like Jimmy Carter, he has successfully mediated intense and complex negotiations, and helped to build hundreds of homes. Like the Dalai Lama and other of the world's greatest preachers, he has a magnificent ability to rally ordinary citizens to see the spiritual wisdom of looking beyond their own well-being to help ensure the well-being of others. I am honored to share a small part of his meditation practice here.

Meditating Can Solve Parenting Problems

There have been several times when I didn't know how to handle a certain parenting situation. When I make some time to pray, meditate, and become quiet, waiting for guidance, the answer always appears. It's not always the answer I expect, but it's always better than I could have ever planned! Things work out better for me when I trust that I will be guided to the perfect answer. There have also been times when, as a mother, I have felt too busy to slow down and go within to receive guidance. It is those times when I could have used Divine direction the most.

One time I was struggling with one of my children. I felt distant and disconnected from my child, and didn't know how to help. We were not communicating well; in fact, we were not communicating much at all. I could tell that he was unhappy and frustrated, but I did not know exactly what was wrong. He was removing himself from anything with the family (I know this can be common with teenagers). I felt a disconcerting feeling in his presence, and it was bothersome because I did not have "solid evidence" of his struggles.

One evening I took time to quiet myself, asking for guidance in helping my child, wanting it to be for the greatest good of everyone involved. The next morning, I woke up, walked downstairs, and clearly saw in my mind's eye that if I turned and looked in the corner of the downstairs guest bathroom, I would find the information I needed. I followed these subtle promptings and sure enough, precisely where I was directed to look, there was evidence of my child's struggle. Just the help I was seeking. Because I had taken time to meditate, pray for guidance, and wait for an answer, I was able to obtain knowledge that helped us to navigate through a difficult time. I approached my child with love and concern. We were able to have honest dialogue about life and the importance of making good choices that will bring about real, lasting happiness. Although there were consequences for his poor behavior, it was ultimately okay because we were able to be open and honest with each other.

Not only can we receive inspiration with regard to our children and family, but we can also receive inspiration and prompting regarding our friends, or any life situation. One day, I was driving home and had a strong inclination that I needed to call one of my girlfriends. I ignored the little nudge to call her, thinking that I really didn't have a purpose for the call, and the timing wasn't ideal for me (I was in the car with all of my children, and it was a bit noisy). Excuses, excuses, excuses. I ignored my inner guidance. Four hours later, I received a call from that same friend. She was very distressed, as her son had been in a serious accident earlier that afternoon. I felt horrible that I did not listen to that quiet, inner voice. I could have been there for her. I made a decision that day: I would never ignore any future promptings I might receive. When we take the time to be introspective, pray, and meditate, we become much more aware of those inner cues.

Introspection is self-observation, self-examination, and self-reflection. The idea dates back to the ancient Greek philosopher, Socrates. He spent much of his life being introspective, as well as encouraging others to do so. Two of Socrates' most well-known quotes are "Know thyself" and "The unexamined life is not worth living." If you feel that you are going without, well, the "fix" is to go within. When things go awry, we try to do something about it: make a plan, push it, pull it, bend it, slam it, curse it, build it, shape it, fix it. Just when we think we have it all figured out, things break down again. Then it's back to the drawing board. If we will take a moment or two to quietly sit, reflect, meditate, and be still, it will open us up to receiving guidance.

Jeanne Ball wrote an article for *The Huffington Post* titled, "Meditating Moms: A Silent Revolution," stating, "More and more mothers are finding meditation to be an effective way to avoid burnout and exhaustion. Rather than taking time out for a coffee, many moms are squeezing in a few minutes of meditation while the baby is napping, or before heading home from work." She continues, "Meditation is especially important for mothers because kids are sensitive to their mothers' stress. Studies show that when a mother is overworked, anxious, or depressed, her children have higher stress, too." Ball quoted a number of mothers in her article who all felt that meditating helped them to remain calm and focused. The article concluded, "Intuition, patience, wisdom, love—all the divine qualities associated with motherhood often depend on how rested we are, how aligned we are with our own inner voice and deepest source of nourishment. With regular meditation, we directly experience our spiritual essence."

When we make time to be introspective, we become more open and receptive to receiving answers we may need in our lives. Ask for internal guidance for what to do next, whom to call, and so forth. When we live our lives being introspective, it also enables us to have the "eyes to see" and the "ears to hear" the messages and answers we may be looking for. In Marianne Williamson's book, *The Law of Divine Compensation,* she shares, "When you meditate and pray, you literally emit different brain waves. You receive impulses of insight and creativity that do not flow easily into an anxious mind." The blessings of being introspective extend far beyond calming the mind. Becoming introspective actually expands the mind. It gives us insight, enlightenment, and awareness. It builds wisdom and tenderness toward others in our human family. It enables us to be the people we wish to be—the people God created us to be.

There are numerous benefits to being introspective and meditating; perhaps this is why it has been around for thousands of years. Meditation is not only associated with feeling less stressed, but also linked to decreased levels of the stress hormone, cortisol. Meditation allows us to get to know our true selves. Researchers from the University of California, Santa Barbara, found that college students who were trained in mindful meditation had a higher level of cognitive function. Have you ever wondered why meditation can make you feel more focused? It is because meditation helps the brain to have better control over processing pain and emotions. Science shows that with a consistent practice of meditation, your brain's emotional processing will benefit, even when you're not actively meditating. Meditation helps you to stay focused, expands your mind, and enhances your overall sense of well-being.

Exercises for building introspection:

- Take time daily to quiet your mind. Sit for ten minutes and clear your mind as much as possible.

- After you have taken a moment to be still, ask a question and wait for the perfect answer.

- I find "Be still and know that I am God" enormously comforting. Sit in stillness, knowing a way will be provided. We don't have to know all the answers.

- The Christian scriptures say we should "pray without ceasing"; one way to accomplish this is to live life in a state of surrender, always knowing that everything we need will be provided.

- Are you feeling scattered? Stressed out? Depressed? Overwhelmed? Then it is time to calm your mind. You don't have to be like Buddha and sit in a perfect lotus position. Just sit comfortably in a chair, or even lie on your back, allowing your mind to be still. Focus all of your attention on your breath. If random thoughts distract you, just tell your thoughts to go away because you are meditating right now, and continue focusing attention on your breath.

thirteen

A conscious mother . . . is mindful.

Mindfulness is simply being aware of what is happening right now without wishing it were different; enjoying the pleasant without holding on when it changes (which it will); being with the unpleasant without fearing it will always be this way (which it won't).

—JAMES BARAZ

By definition, *being mindful* means to be attentive, inclined to be aware, careful, and considerate. This attention leads to a clear awareness of our thoughts as well as our environment; now we can observe with loving kindness what is happening around us. Instead of judging, we view these thoughts as fleeting and inconsequential. This does not mean disconnection from life; rather, the mind is actively engaged and flexible. When we are mindful, we see another's needs and feel the desire to reach out, extending love, support, and compassion.

While mindfulness and presence are very similar, there are significant differences. In mindfulness practice, we are focusing on the substance of our moment-to-moment experience. When we practice presence, we are not really concerned with the substance of our experience; we're neither focusing on it nor trying to block it out. So, a practice in presence is much more about letting go of the need to grasp, to understand, to be preoccupied with anything, and simply relaxing into the openness of our being. A practice in mindfulness is a heightened awareness about the essence of each moment.

Our culture has a difficult time understanding the value of mindfulness because we're so preoccupied with the busyness of doing, acquiring, achieving, and progressing. Even our leisure time is spent being busy *and* mindless (reality TV, anyone?).

People don't make the effort to think or be mindful anymore. So much of our culture is automated, helping to free up our time so we don't have to think about simple, mundane tasks anymore. As a result, our children lack the training to keep their minds focused and attentive. Information, entertainment, and virtually anything we need is instantly available, without much thinking required. Kids, who used to be outside more often, enjoying nature and connecting with one another, sit slumped for hours staring at the TV, playing video games, going on Twitter and Facebook, tapping away mindlessly on their smartphones, eyes glazed over. We as parents have become equally disconnected from reality and the present moment, rolling through our days on autopilot, watching our own TVs or computer screens (what we call "relaxation"). In many ways, we are all living a virtual life.

Living a virtual life has its consequences. Virtual reality takes away the aspect of social life in its formation and maintenance of interpersonal relationships. Virtual interaction now takes the place of belonging to community. Living a virtual life can lead to low self-esteem and feelings of worthlessness and insignificance. A plethora of stimulation is just a click or a touch screen away, ensuring that even the slightest trace of boredom will never set in. Researchers for the children's charity Kidscape accessed the online activities of 2,300 eleven- to eighteen-year-olds in the UK and found that 45 percent of them said they were sometimes happier online than in their real lives. One of the participants in the study told researchers, "It is easier to be who you want to be, because nobody knows you, and if you don't like the situation you can just exit and it is over." Another participant reflected, "You can say anything online. You can talk to people that you don't normally speak to, and you can edit your pictures so you look better. It is as if you are a completely different person."

Can you see the danger in living a virtual life? Mindfulness is the antidote. Mindfulness is a skill that needs to be cultivated. Recent brain-imaging studies reveal that sections of our brains are highly active during downtime. This has led scientists to suggest that moments of "not-doing" are critical for synthesizing and connecting new information, ideas, and experiences. Dr. Michael Rich, a professor at Harvard Medical School, explained it this way in a 2010 *New York Times* article: "Downtime is to the brain what sleep is to the body." In the past thirty years or so, our consumption of information has increased by leaps and bounds, while our downtime continues to shrink. *New York Times* best-selling author of *The Divine Matrix*, Gregg Braden, observes, "We are drowning in information, while starving for wisdom."

In the midst of this glut of information, our need for mindfulness and focused attention is growing. More than 40 percent of our actions are based on habits, not conscious decisions. The practice of mindfulness can help to counteract the idea of simply living our lives on autopilot. "Mindfulness practice," according to Jon Kabat-Zinn, a pioneer in mindfulness-based stress reduction, "means that we commit fully in each moment to be present; inviting ourselves to interface with this moment in full awareness, with the intention to embody as best we can an orientation of calmness, mindfulness, and equanimity right here and right now."

Living with Purpose
Life can feel like an avalanche of things to do—the cell phone constantly beeping, a barrage of activities to complete, work deadlines to meet, and on and on. The busyness of life can take us away from being mindful, from thinking before we act. When we are mindful, we live our lives with purpose as opposed to living out our days in rote mode.

One evening I was lying in bed with my six-year-old daughter, Lola, trying to help her fall asleep. She was holding my hand when she said, "Mom, my teacher needs a volunteer to come into our class and work with us on our spelling words. Will you do it?" I answered quickly, explaining that it would be difficult for me because I am unable to drive, and would need help with my wheelchair and other logistics.

She broke down in tears, sobbing, and said, "I wish you could walk." We lay there together for quite a while. She shared with me how difficult it was for her to be six, and to have to do so many things by herself. She just wanted me to be able to participate more in her life. I acknowledged how difficult that must be for her, and snuggled with her while she drifted off to sleep.

I decided that night, come hell or high water, I was going to be in that first-grade classroom in the morning. I got up early, made arrangements for my husband to drop me off with the kids, and spent the morning with Lola and her classmates. Out of the corner of my eye, I could see Lola beaming. She was so proud to have her mother there in her class. At dinner that evening, she made an announcement to the family: "Today was the best day of my life because Mom came to my class." Although it took a tremendous effort on my part to be there, it made a world of difference to Lola. As mothers, we can be more attentive, aware, and considerate of our children's needs. We can make an effort to be more mindful. Small, simple acts of mindfulness can make a world of difference to a child. By being mindful, I was able to help Lola feel loved, valued, and important.

Mothering is a constant balancing act. Being mindful allows us to prioritize with ease what is really important. Sometimes our own needs should come first, exemplified by the familiar flight attendant's message ("Put on your own oxygen mask first before you assist your child"). And sometimes our children's needs should be met first. When we are mindful, it helps us to be more open and trusting, and to have greater levels of empathy and compassion.

Empathy is the heart of emotional intelligence, hardwiring the brain for self-control and higher cognition. Empathy involves acceptance. This moment is as it is; we cannot change it, manipulate it, or disagree with it. Empathy helps our children to accept and process their own feelings, and teaches them how to handle their disappointment and frustration. If we cannot accept the moment as it is, it creates resistance and upset, leaving us unable to give empathy.

In her curriculum on conscious discipline, Becky Bailey, PhD, observes that the desire to be understood is a powerful human behavior. It is one of our most basic needs. Think about this: Every war, along with every fight in every home, has its roots in a lack of empathy. Without empathy, we will destroy one another; with empathy, we create oneness, where attack is impossible. Integrating mindfulness into our lives and the lives of our children will stimulate empathy.

Right now, I cannot be as physically involved with parenting my children as I would like, but when I practice mindfulness, it helps me tap into knowing what is really important to my children. For example, recently my son finished a grueling college summer class. In spite of the fact that I was not able to "help" him in any way during the summer semester, I was able to acknowledge and celebrate the successful completion of his class. I simply sent him a text message, letting him know I thought he was doing a fabulous job, that I admired his ambition, and that I was proud of his hard work. I knew how important this class was to my son, and that he'd had to sacrifice most of his summer fun for school. He replied, "Thank you, Mom. I really, really appreciate the recognition." Although we enjoyed a movie together that weekend, to give him a break and celebrate his success, the most significant thing I did for Scott was the text message I sent of love and acknowledgment.

Part of living is eating, so let's talk about eating with purpose. We can even be more mindful when we eat. "Mindful eating" helps us to pay attention to the signals our body sends us when we are eating. We can nonjudgmentally focus on where, when, and why we eat. By listening to our body's cues to evaluate what is driving us to eat, it helps us to determine if we are truly hungry. When we are mindful when we eat, it helps us to slow down and really enjoy our food. Research shows that mindful eating can lead to weight loss and maintenance. That is a plus!

Getting in Touch with Our Authentic Selves

The practice of mindfulness allows for looking deeply into our own experience and ultimately revealing the essence of our authentic nature. The practice of mindfulness will help us open up and access the goodness of our authentic nature, which is always present.

A study published in the journal *Perspectives on Psychological Science* illustrates how mindfulness can help us to know ourselves without the negative or positive bias. Mindfulness allows us to see our authentic selves in two ways: nonjudgmental observation, and attention. Nonjudgmental observation enables people to get to know themselves without feeling any negative feelings.

In a recent study conducted by the University of Utah, researchers showed that mindfulness is linked with greater emotional stability and self-control, not to mention better sleep. Boy, if that's what mindfulness can do for my children and me, I will practice it! "People who reported higher levels of mindfulness described better control over their emotions and behaviors during the day," researcher Holly Rau said. "In addition, higher mindfulness was associated with lower activation at bedtime, which could have benefits for sleep quality and future ability to manage stress."

Mindfulness is about bringing attention to every situation and focusing on all five senses. What do we hear? What do we smell? Taste? Feel? See? When we choose to live in this manner, literally everything gives us an opportunity to be mindful. Whether we are brushing our teeth, walking the dog, washing dishes, or making the bed, we can be mindful and present as we focus on each of our senses while accomplishing each task.

While it's important for us as parents to be mindful, we can also teach our children to appreciate the benefits of mindfulness. Being mindful is especially important for our children when they are doing their homework and studying for school. Bringing mindful attention to schoolwork will reduce anxiety and keep them in the present moment, focusing only on the task at hand instead of feeling overwhelmed by a heavy homework load. Mindfulness will also help our children to have a greater capacity to retain the materials they are studying.

Dealing with Interruptions

I think we would all agree that it's rude to interrupt someone before he or she finishes speaking, interrupt a perfectly good meal by taking a cell-phone call, or interrupt your daughter as she shares with you the important aspects of her day. Our thoughts can also interrupt our mindfulness. They can generate momentum, leaping from one thought to another like a grasshopper. We can limit the interruption of our thoughts by consciously focusing on being mindful.

Recently I was riding in the golf cart while my son and husband were golfing. Because I was writing this chapter, my thoughts were focused on the topic of being mindful. As I observed the two of them golfing, I noticed that they were not only present to their game, but also mindful of how they would play each stroke. They were mindful of one another, the length of the hole, the hazards, sand traps, and bunkers—even the slight breeze. Aware of all aspects of their game, they would carefully select the perfect club and approach their next shot thoughtfully. As mothers, if we can practice bringing mindful attention to our lives just like a professional golfer brings to the course, we will become more attentive and in touch with the needs of our children, and much less distracted by typical interruptions.

Exercises for growing more mindful:

- Before sitting down to watch TV, put some thought into the programming you will watch. Choose shows that are uplifting and have a positive message. Select shows that are mindful and have purpose.

- Become aware of your child's needs, and make an effort to meet them.

- Read Jon Kabat-Zinn's book, *Coming to Our Senses: Healing Ourselves and the World through Mindfulness.*

- Try one of these as a remedy to become more mindful: slow down, make eye contact, or go outside and play.

- Ask your child the all-important question: "What do you need?" This will give her the opportunity to stop and think, to be mindful about her response. It increases the chances for good communication, too.

- Notice where you tend to zone out (for example, when driving, e-mailing, texting, surfing the web, feeding the dog, doing dishes, brushing teeth, and so on). Practice bringing more awareness to those activities.

- When eating your next meal, use all of your senses—smelling, seeing, tasting, hearing, and feeling. This will help you to slow down, really enjoy your food, and only eat what your body needs.

fourteen

A conscious mother . . .
is a student and a teacher.

A hundred years from now, it will not matter what kind of car I drove, what kind of house I lived in, how much money I had in the bank . . . but the world may be a better place because I made a difference in the life of a child.

—FOREST WITCRAFT

A good friend once said to me, "You can't give what you don't have. If you don't have a million dollars, you can't give a million dollars." This idea is so simple and so true. If we are not trying to improve and to learn more ourselves, how can we expect to teach our children? I am constantly reading books and articles, listening to inspiring talks, and learning new things. When I encounter something valuable, I share it with my children. Thus, the student becomes the teacher.

It is essential to expand our minds and continue learning. You do not have to spend your life in a classroom to be a lifelong learner. There is nothing wrong with taking a class, but there is a lot to be learned from everyday life and the world around us. Have a conversation with a friend, watch TV, read a book or a magazine, browse the Internet for an interesting article; it doesn't matter how you choose to learn—it just matters that you do. Henry Ford once said, "Anyone who stops learning is old, whether at twenty or eighty. Anyone who keeps learning stays young. The greatest thing in life is to keep your mind young." The world keeps changing. It is important to keep learning so you can keep up, especially because our children are learning every day. We have all heard that you can't teach an old dog new tricks; well, that's just not true.

At the National Prayer Breakfast, Dr. Benjamin Carson, pediatric neurosurgeon at Johns Hopkins Hospital, gave the keynote address. He spoke about the importance of educating ourselves, stating, "Two hundred years ago when slavery was going on it was illegal to educate a slave, particularly to teach him to read. Why do you think that was? Because when you educate a man, you liberate a man." He continued: "It is important to develop your mind because then you have control of your own life."

I have learned that life will support me daily with exactly what I need. As my disability has set in, I have become an observer of life as opposed to an active participant. As my life was shifting to that of becoming more of an observer, I began to develop a fear that others would leave me behind. I worried that as they went about their lives as usual, I would be left alone, unable to join them in typical parenting activities. At times, I have felt alone now that I can no longer participate in certain activities with my family, friends, and loved ones. It is important for me to remember that God will never leave me. He is always with me, and so I am never completely alone.

Sharing Life's Lessons

One spring break our family took a trip to Palm Springs, California. We were there to enjoy the beautiful warm weather, to hike, bike, roller-skate, golf, and play tennis, and I was unable to physically participate in any of the activities. One afternoon, we planned a trip to the swimming pool. I was going as a spectator, looking forward to watching my girls have fun swimming with their dad. When the time came, I was unable to join my family due to exhaustion and some physical struggles I was having at the time. It just wasn't going to happen for me. The girls all said, "It's okay; we'll stay home with you." With sadness in my heart, I put a smile on my face and insisted they go and have a good time. Just because I was immobile didn't mean they had to stop living and experiencing life.

They left to enjoy the pool. Instead of feeling sorry for myself, I decided to sit on the back patio and soak in the beautiful sunset, meditate, and contemplate my life. Just as I sat down in my lounge chair, I noticed a mallard duck off in the distance, wandering in my direction. The duck waddled across the golf course and right up to where I was sitting. I greeted him, and he quacked back. Then a miracle happened; the little duck sat down adjacent to me, both of us looking out across the lush, green golf course facing the sunset. There we sat together, the duck never leaving my side. We continued to sit and enjoy each other's company. The mallard's "wife" waddled up to him and aggressively quacked her obvious disapproval; he responded with a quack, and she swiftly waddled away. After keeping me company for about forty minutes, my new feathered friend suddenly rose from my side and left. Less than one minute later my family walked through the front door, returning from their fun at the pool.

I was not alone. I knew this duck was sent to keep me company during a sad, lonely time. I was the student, and I learned that God will never leave me alone. His love and presence are always with me. I told my children about my feathered companion, teaching them that God loves us and will never allow us to feel alone. Once again, I was a student of life, becoming a teacher as I shared my experience with my children.

A good teacher clarifies her own ideas and strengthens them by teaching them. A good teacher must believe in the ideas she is teaching; conviction will be lacking unless we share what we've learned. It is important to believe in the students (our children) to whom we are offering our ideas. We must be patient as we continually teach our children. Learning means change, which some people resist because it feels uncomfortable. Don't be surprised if your children resist learning and applying something new in their lives. Teaching and learning are our biggest strengths, enabling us to create change in our lives. As mothers, we hope to teach our children so much that eventually, they will no longer need us as teachers; they will be able to stand on their own.

We Are Models of Behavior for Our Children

As mothers, we have been entrusted with the responsibility of teaching truths and values to our children. It is our responsibility to nurture and teach the next generation. "We are here to take care of the children; it's just that every child on the planet is one of our children. We are here to take care of the home, but this entire Earth is our home. So this archetype of the woman as the mother of the species [is true]; you see this in every advanced mammalian species. If you don't take care of the babies, then that species does not necessarily survive," Marianne Williamson told Oprah Winfrey recently on *Super Soul Sunday*. The health of any society, the happiness of its people, and their prosperity and peace all find common roots in how the children are taught in the home. This takes mindful parenting—one book read aloud, one meal spent together, one simple conversation at a time. Conscientious, consistent parenting is one of the most powerful forces for good in the world. We must be aware of what we are teaching our children.

Even when I don't think I'm teaching, I have realized that I am always teaching my children simply because they observe my behaviors and actions. It truly is a full-time job. Recently, this point was made very clear when my husband took our youngest daughter with him to run a few errands after school. They had to stop by the office supply store, the bank, and the gas station. While at the gas station, the two of them went inside the mini market for a cool drink. They noticed fresh-baked donuts and simply couldn't resist. While packing up the donuts, my husband took one of the maple bars and enjoyed a bite. It was so delicious that Chris and Lola devoured the entire thing, right there in the mini market. They went up to the checkout stand, paid for their treats, and climbed back in the car. On their drive home, Chris remembered and announced, "Oh no, Lola! I forgot to pay for the donut we ate. I need to go back and pay for it."

He dropped Lola off at the house where she quickly found me in my office. She beamed as she started to recount her day, telling me about school and what she had for lunch, and then her fun adventure with Dad.

"I got to run errands with Daddy!" Lola said. "We went to the office supply store and the bank. I got a lollipop at the bank; I picked the red one, because cherry is my favorite. Then we went to the gas station. Dad is so much fun! We ate a maple donut right there in the store." Then she continued, "Mom, we left the store and forgot to pay for the donut we ate. But you know what? Dad said he would go back and pay for it."

What Lola said next made me realize that we are always teaching our children simply by the way we live our lives.

With deep respect, admiration, and love for her dad, Lola shared, "I just *knew* Daddy would go back."

Chris had no idea his youngest daughter was watching him so closely to see how he would handle the situation. Unbeknownst to him, he was teaching Lola a great lesson on the importance of being honest. Clearly, the greatest teaching moments are not necessarily when we formally sit down and teach a principle to our child; they are more often made up of the subtle choices we make in our daily lives.

I am always amazed when my children share with me a situation they are dealing with in their lives and they say, "Mom, one time you said . . ." And then they continue to quote me on something that I previously have shared with them. I usually cannot recall the quote, and think to myself, "Well, I better be real careful about what I say, because they just might listen."

Our children are like little sponges. They really do soak up everything we do and say in our daily lives. We may not always be aware of it, but they learn through our example, and not necessarily by what we tell them. If we tell our child not to raise her voice yet we are always yelling, chances are they will learn an undesirable communicating skill, believing that they need to shout to be heard. When you are always being watched, your kids are gathering lessons, whether intentional or not. As parents, we are responsible to teach our children—sometimes through our example, and sometimes through our words. If I attend a movie I've forbidden my children to see, my parental credibility will be diminished in their eyes. If I expect my children to be honest, I must be honest. If I expect my children to have a good work ethic, I must have a good work ethic. If I expect my children to be honorable, I must be honorable.

Exercises for being a student and teacher of life:

- Read one inspiring book, article, or e-mail this week. Share what you have learned with your children.

- Pay close attention to the life lessons you are learning daily. Share those lessons with your children.

- Be aware and make a conscious choice to live your life with impeccable integrity. The way you live your life will provide the greatest teaching moments for your children.

- Take joy in the simple things. Kids today are bombarded by materialistic messages; it is easy for them to think that their happiness depends on something outside of themselves. Demonstrate that the best things in life are free. For your next birthday, instead of asking for a gift from the store, tell your children you would prefer just spending time with them, cooking a meal, enjoying a picnic in the park, or going for a hike. Or simply ask them to write you a thoughtful birthday card.

- Keep your word. Remember, your words have extraordinary power with your children. Our children will learn to be trustworthy through our example of being trustworthy. If you make a promise, follow through.

fifteen

A conscious mother . . .
is a model of gratitude.

As we express our gratitude, we must never forget that the highest appreciation is not to utter words, but to live by them.

—JOHN F. KENNEDY

One day I received an e-mail containing a link to a clip of crickets chirping. The crickets were chirping at regular speed at first, and then the chirping slowed down to the same speed of a human life. The outcome was remarkable. It sounded like a beautiful chorus singing. The message was about singing praises of gratitude. It made me think, *Do I go through my day complaining, or do I sing praises of gratitude for all of my many blessings?*

I have to admit, I was waking up every day complaining, "This is hard. I am tired. I don't want to do this today." My mind chatter continued even when my mouth was quiet. *Poor me, poor me, poor me!* After listening to the sound of crickets singing praise, I reexamined the song coming from my heart. Now I wake up saying *Thank you,* choosing to see all of the many blessings in my life, big and small. We only need the "eyes to see and the ears to hear" all of the miracles around us. The miracles are always there, and by developing gratitude, we will see them even more.

Sometimes life feels so difficult that it's hard to have gratitude for our challenges. Gratitude is key to living out all of our wishes and ambitions. A practice of gratitude helps to strengthen feelings of joy and well-being. To harness the power of gratitude it must be part of our daily regimen. Developing gratitude helps us to overcome self-pity and misfortune, and it keeps our focus on the exceptional and magnificent things in our lives. Gratitude also helps us keep things in perspective. Unleash the power of gratitude and create a more peaceful, abundant life.

Modeling Gratitude for Your Child

Modeling a life lived in gratitude will encourage an attitude of gratitude in your children. The results are beautiful. Your children will learn to be thankful for what they have in life. How refreshing! So many kids live from a sense of entitlement and expectation; the antidote is to teach our children gratitude. They often want what their friends have, whether it's the latest fashion or electronic gadget. We need to teach them that these things are not important, and that so many people in the world have so much less. Our children can easily see if we are thankful for the blessings that come into our life, and whether we give thanks and show appreciation for those blessings. When we model this, we reinforce the behavior and the importance of that behavior.

In the introduction of this book I shared my experience of gratitude, or lack thereof. It feels appropriate to share it again in this chapter. It has been difficult for me to feel thankful for my MS. How could I ever feel happy or grateful for becoming immobile and disabled? Many things have since led me to a place where I can finally feel gratitude for my health challenge. As I've mentioned, the experience has forced me to slow down and realize that my future would not be the one I'd envisioned—that of a busy mom, physically engaged in my family's activities. I have had plenty of time to be still—to pray, meditate, and receive inspiration. Now I can see that all along, I have been the recipient of constant love and support, enabling me to do what I really *need* to do. Today, I can see the blessings through my hardships. It's easy to feel thankful when life is going our way; the question is, can we still carry a grateful heart when life is difficult?

Feeling gratitude can be as simple as a matter of perspective. Is the glass half empty or half full? When was the last time you were truly, truly grateful for your home, the bed you sleep in, your lungs to breathe, or your eyes to see? It is common to take the simple, everyday blessings in our lives for granted.

In her book *The Hiding Place,* Corrie ten Boom was able to feel gratitude even in the most horrific circumstances. She and her sister Betsie had been imprisoned by the Nazis for hiding Jews behind the wall of their Holland home. The Nazi prison conditions were intolerable, and Corrie wrote about them in her book:

Barracks 8 was in the quarantine compound. Next to us—perhaps as a deliberate warning to newcomers—were located the punishment barracks. From there, all day long and often into the night, came the sounds of hell itself. They were not the sounds of anger, or of any human emotion, but of a cruelty altogether detached: blows landing in regular rhythm, screams keeping pace. We would stand in our ten-deep ranks with our hands trembling at our sides, longing to jam them against our ears, to make the sounds stop.

It grew harder and harder. Even within these four walls there was too much misery, too much seemingly pointless suffering. Every day something else failed to make sense, something else grew too heavy.

Yet, in the midst of the suffering, the women prisoners around Corrie and Betsie found comfort in the little Bible studies they held in the barracks. Corrie wrote that they gathered around the Bible "like waifs clustered around a blazing fire. . . . The blacker the night around us grew, the brighter and truer and more beautiful burned the Word of God."

When they were moved to Barracks 28, Corrie was horrified by the fact that their reeking, straw-bed platforms swarmed with fleas. How could they live in such a place? It was Betsie who discovered the answer: They would express gratitude in all things. They thanked God for the fact they were together. They were grateful they had a Bible. They were even grateful for the horrible crowds of prisoners, because it meant that more people would be able to hear God's Word. And then, Betsie thanked God for the fleas. In fact, while the fleas were a nuisance, they were also a blessing. The women were able to have Bible studies in the barracks with a great deal of freedom, never bothered by supervisors coming in and harassing them. They finally discovered that it was the fleas that kept the supervisors out. Dozens of desperate women were thus free to hear the comforting, hope-giving Word of God, protected from unspeakable abuse and torture.

It is easy to show gratitude when things are going well in our lives; it's much harder to appreciate the things that are obviously horrible, unpleasant, even painful. But sometimes even seemingly negative things have a purpose, and we can learn from them.

Do You Have a Grateful Parenting Style?

In raising children to have gratitude, we need to examine our parenting style. Are we a service/product provider instead of a parent? When we are all about providing service for our family, our children become consumers instead of part of the family team. As parents, we work hard to provide the best for our family, but our children can become ungrateful, expecting more and more while making little or no effort to contribute. This parenting style robs our children of the basic human need of feeling that they are important and valued members of the family. It breeds dependency instead of loving appreciation. To help our children develop gratitude and appreciation, we must give our kids opportunities to help out around the house. Our children then become producers instead of consumers. They become contributing members of the family.

During the summer months, I give each of my children the opportunity to plan and prepare one family meal a week. This gives them a chance to learn how to create a menu by looking for what is on sale, and in season. They also learn that it's important for the meal to be not only delicious and nutritious, but also pleasing to the eye. After they create the menu, we go to the grocery store and select the items they need. When it's their turn to cook for the family, they work hard to prep and prepare a delicious meal. Not only are they learning the important skills of menu preparation, grocery shopping, and preparing and cooking food, but also the valuable lesson of how much effort it takes to feed a family. When our children participate in planning and preparing family meals, they have deeper gratitude for every meal provided for them, because they know how much effort it takes.

A simple way to show gratitude is through appreciation. Take time to thank someone for the little ways they may help you: passing you something you can't reach, opening a door, picking up something you may have dropped. Recently I heard a story about a gentleman who took time to write a special thank-you note to his favorite grade-school teacher. When she received it, she replied, "Dear John: You will never know how much your letter meant to me. I am eighty-three years old, and I am living all alone in one room. My friends are all gone. My family's gone. I taught for fifty years, and yours is the first thank-you letter I have ever gotten from a student. Sometimes I wonder what I did with my life. I will read and reread your letter until the day I die." Because of this man's appreciation, his childhood teacher now understands the impact her life has had on another. Imagine how you would feel if you received an unexpected letter of thanks from someone you had no idea you'd helped.

Exercises for fostering gratitude in your family:

- Keep a gratitude journal. Each day, list five things you are grateful for. When we live our days knowing that we need to list a few things we are grateful for, we tend to live each day more aware of all of our blessings.

- Sit down with your family, and together, make a list of everything you're grateful for. We had a fun challenge in our family. If an item was left off the list, they couldn't use it for twenty-four hours. My daughters were quick to include the telephone, food, water, electricity, and the toilet!

- Google "crickets' chirping slowed down," and listen to the crickets' song of praise. Examine the song coming from your heart. Make sure it is a song of gratitude and praise.

- Make a list of all the jobs and tasks it takes to keep the family going. Be sure to add "making money and paying bills" to the list. Now, review the list with your children and divide it among all the family members. This will give your children an opportunity to contribute to the family, understand that they are an important part of the whole, and realize just what it takes to make a family run smoothly.

- Have your child be responsible for making dinner one night a week. He will be excited to plan the menu, shop for the food items, and prep and cook the meal. He will be learning important life skills, including gratitude for the meals that are prepared for him, and you'll get the night off from cooking. Remember to have him participate in the cleanup afterward.

- Think of someone who has positively influenced your life. Take some time to write them a thank-you note, expressing your gratitude and appreciation for the impact they've had on your life. No doubt they will feel honored and appreciated.

sixteen

A conscious mother . . .
sets a loving tone in her home.

A house is built of walls and beams; a home is built with love and dreams.

—ANONYMOUS

I am a firm believer that the mother sets the tone for her home and family. We have a great influence on the atmosphere set in our home simply by our attitude and example. It has been my experience that if I am frustrated, impatient, angry, and yelling, or loving, calm, patient, and soft-spoken, it all directly affects the mood in our home. Life can seem overwhelming at times, and we may not necessarily be able to control our environment, but we can always control how we choose to respond and react in any given situation.

One busy morning, as the kids were getting ready to leave for school, we were all rushed. "Hurry, get your backpack! Where are your shoes? Did you remember your lunch? Hurry, you're going to be late! What about your teeth; did you brush? Come on, hurry!" I was like a crazy woman ordering my kids to hurry, hurry, hurry! By the time they were ready to step out the door, we were all frustrated and angry. I gave them a quick kiss good-bye and blurted out "I love you" as I sent them on their way. I didn't feel good when they left, and I'm sure they didn't feel loved; they were probably happy to be away from me. I decided in that moment that I would never create that feeling in my home again, and, especially, I would never send my children out into the world feeling frustrated by my behavior. I would choose to show up for my family in a calm, loving, patient way. I thought to myself, *Does it really matter if they are tardy, or if they didn't brush their teeth or hair one day?* When looking at the big picture, all of those little details are not important. But the way we behave and speak to our children has a huge impact on their day. I am not purporting that we make it a practice of not having good personal hygiene or being organized and prepared for the day, but those things are secondary to how we treat one another.

The next morning we were just as busy as the prior day, but this morning we had a different experience. Before going to bed that evening, I asked myself, "How am I going to accomplish this and create a peaceful home?" It was going to be my responsibility to be better organized and prepared, and to allow enough time to get the kids ready and out the door without feeling rushed. Not much was different—we couldn't find one shoe, the lunches were not packed, and teeth needed to be brushed—but I decided to speak to my children in a calm tone, making sure they felt happy and loved when they left our home. It was a much better way to start the day. The morning was still somewhat hectic, but my children began their day feeling valued and loved, messy hair and all. My family does not feel as rushed when I am better prepared and give myself extra time to get ready for the day.

We create the emotional weather in our home, and, much like the flap of butterfly wings, our personal climate can dramatically change the emotional weather patterns in our home. A busy day with children provides many opportunities for us to practice our calm emotional-weather climate, and it's easy to fall from grace. All of our relationships offer us so many chances for growth. If you are feeling triggered by your spouse, a challenging situation, or a difficult person, and anger arises in you, it is easy to swallow it and pretend that everything is okay. However, anger is a hot emotion, and much like the warm pressure system building over the ocean, it needs to be released. We need to find appropriate ways to allow our anger to escape. Meditation, prayer, daily spiritual reading, uplifting music, and exercise can help us to shift focus. It is healthy and important to go within and turn toward the anger, allowing it to express itself with whatever needs to be said. Now, this is not a blame game: "He always . . ." Or, "He never . . ." You may begin there, but listen to your words and place it in an "I" statement: "He never listens to me!" should be rephrased as "I don't feel heard." Turn to the part of you that does not feel heard and speak to it yourself: "I hear you, and understand that you are not feeling heard." Turning toward your feelings and giving them a voice releases the anger. This is similar to a pressure valve that gently lets off steam, offering us the space to hear what our needs are, and to express them with love and kindness, not through anger. By acknowledging and validating our authentic feelings, it allows us to move through heavy emotions in a healthy manner, choosing the tone we would like to set for our home.

Some mothers have a quick temper and a short fuse—yelling, ranting, and raving to express themselves. This is unsettling, and feels unsafe for our children. Other mothers can be completely out of touch with their own feelings, and if something feels off or uncomfortable, they push the negative feelings down and just try to be happy. This is not healthy either. When we do not feel, acknowledge, and express our genuine emotions, this negative energy stays trapped in our bodies, making us physically ill. Take time to check in with yourself daily. Be sure to acknowledge your true feelings and express them in a healthy and loving way.

It has only been in recent years that I've learned to feel what I really feel. It is easy for me to be happy and joyful. I used to think "Water off a duck's back" if something was upsetting to me. Rather than acknowledge the negative emotion, feel it, and give it a voice, I would put on a happy face and get on with my day. There is nothing wrong with being joyful and happy; in fact, these are desirable traits. But we should never abandon ourselves or become invisible, invalidating our feelings. Acknowledge your true feelings, express them in a healthy and loving way, and set the tone you would like to enjoy in your home.

Creating a Loving Environment

As mothers, it is our responsibility to create a safe, loving home environment where all members feel valued, loved, and respected. As a teenager, I remember enjoying being in our home. This was important, because I knew if my friends were making choices that I did not want to participate in, I could always hang out at my house. It was a happy, safe, and loving environment. I didn't feel the need to go out; I was perfectly happy being at home with my family. My mother created that joyful, happy environment, surrounding us with uplifting books, music, TV, and entertainment. She would not allow any contention in our home, and was quick to put a stop to quarreling or negativity.

The time we spend in our homes and the environment we create there has a powerful influence on our children. This is where our children learn how to behave, and where they learn important life skills.

If a child lives with criticism, he
    learns to condemn.
If a child lives with hostility, he
    learns to fight.
If a child lives with ridicule, he
    learns to be shy.
If a child lives with shame, he learns
    to feel guilty.
If a child lives with tolerance, he
    learns to be patient.
If a child lives with encouragement,
    he learns confidence.
If a child lives with praise, he learns
    to appreciate.

If a child lives with fairness, he
  learns justice.
If a child lives with security, he
  learns to have faith.
If a child lives with approval, he
  learns to like himself.
If a child lives with acceptance and
  friendship, he learns to find love
  in the world.

—Children Learn What They Live © 1963
by John Philip Co.

It is sufficient to say that a person has a significant advantage in life if they come from a loving, supportive home. Many people are still successful even though they came from a less than desirable upbringing. But, having our basic needs met and knowing we are loved and supported makes the challenges of day-to-day life that much easier to face. As mothers, we have the exciting opportunity to powerfully influence the success of our children simply by the loving environment we establish daily in our home. Having a solid and stable home is the nucleus and core foundation on which our child's physical, emotional, and intellectual development is built.

In an ideal environment, parents remain constant and stay connected, helping their children build trusting relationships. A well-balanced and secure home reliably provides warmth, emotional support, and day-to-day nurturing. Securely attached children are better off in all aspects—socially, emotionally, and academically. Insecurity creeps in when children feel unsafe and fail to understand or foresee their parents' moods. A constant, predictable, calm, loving home will build a child's confidence and help her to self-govern effectively. Remember to take 100 percent self-responsibility for your moods and behaviors, aiding your child to feel greater levels of safety, security, and confidence.

The Power of the Spoken Word

The following story illustrates this concept of setting a loving tone beautifully. One of the few women who survived an Auschwitz concentration camp was fifteen years old and her brother was eight when they lost their parents. As she and her brother were on the train going to Auschwitz, she looked down and noticed her little brother's shoes were missing. She said, "You are so stupid! Can't you keep your things together? For goodness' sake!" She spoke to him the way an older sister might speak to a younger brother. Unfortunately, it was the last thing she would ever say to her little brother because she never saw him again; he did not survive. When she came out of Auschwitz, she made a vow: "I will never say anything that cannot stand as the last thing I ever say." We should all take on this vow, and do our best to speak only kind and loving words.

We've all heard the old adage, "Sticks and stones may break my bones, but words will never hurt me." Who came up with that one? It is not true! You can heal pretty easily from an injury caused by sticks and stones. It is the unkind words we speak that cut so deep it can take a lifetime to heal, damaging a person's soul.

In his book *The Four Agreements,* Don Miguel Ruiz explains the significance of the spoken word. A single word can be powerful enough to change—even destroy—a life. The human mind is like fertile ground; when you plant the seed, it will grow. The spoken word is like a seed planted in the mind. What kind of seeds are you planting in your child's mind? Are you planting seeds of love, or fear? Recently, my daughter picked up her class schedule for the new school year. When comparing her classes and teachers with her friends, everyone had their own personal opinion. "Wow, you have that teacher? She is so great. Everyone loves her," or "Oh no! You have that teacher? He's the worst! Getting a C in his class is like getting an A in any other class." Can you see the effect these words can have on influencing my daughter's opinion about her teachers? Without ever meeting her new teachers, she has formed an opinion based on someone else's experience. Don Miguel Ruiz suggests we be impeccable with our words. By being carefully selective with our words and the tone in which we speak, we can consciously create a loving environment in our home.

To illustrate the power of our words, we look to Dr. Masaru Emoto. Through the 1990s Dr. Emoto performed a series of experiments observing the physical effects of words, prayers, music, and environment on the crystalline structure of water. Dr. Emoto hired photographers to take pictures of water after it was exposed to the different variables and subsequently frozen so that they would form crystalline structures. The results were nothing short of remarkable. The water that was positively spoken to was far more symmetrical and aesthetically pleasing than the water that was stamped with dark, negative phrases. We already know the influence positive or negative thinking can have on the surrounding environment. Now we have tangible evidence that the words we speak impact the crystalline structure of water. When Dr. Emoto used a negative phrase like "You make me sick," the structure of the water was chaotic and ugly, shaped like a blob. When Dr. Emoto used a loving phrase, such as "Thank you," or "I love you," the water structure was uniform and beautiful, similar to an intricate snowflake. If words can have a dramatic impact on a water molecule, think of the impact our words have on our children. Our words have the power to positively or negatively influence the life of our child.

Exercises for creating a loving home environment:

- When life seems overwhelming, take a deep breath and decide to respond in a loving, calm manner.

- Too many mothers yell at their kids. Do not yell. Always choose to speak to your children in a way that generates love and respect. Some may think this is impossible, but my mother raised six kids, and I have never heard her raise her voice. It *is* possible.

- Before reacting to your child's questionable behavior, ask yourself: Is this the way I would like to be treated?

- Be clear when expressing your requests, desires, and needs to your children. Have them repeat back to you what you are requesting.

- Instead of having the TV blaring in the background, play uplifting music, especially when working around the house. Snow White and the Seven Dwarfs had it right with the song "Whistle While You Work." Music makes even the mundane enjoyable.

- When you speak to your children—or anyone, for that matter—ask yourself: "Can this stand as the last thing I ever say to this person?"

seventeen

A conscious mother . . . understands the importance of human touch.

You can't wrap love in a box, but you can wrap a person in a hug.

—AUTHOR UNKNOWN

After a long day, my body was exhausted; I lay down on the couch, unable to sit up, roll over, or move. The fatigue was so overwhelming that I was having a difficult time even raising my arms. Lola, who was six years old at the time, arrived home from school, missing me, and was equally tired from her day as a first grader. She wanted some love and attention, so snuggled up next to me on the couch. At that moment, I had nothing to give her, and felt a sense of inadequacy as a mother. But while I couldn't raise my arms to play with her hair or tickle her back, I could snuggle next to her and flop my arm over her body. She cuddled up to me and quickly calmed down, telling me how much she loved it when I hugged her. Although I felt inadequate, that was all she needed. The simplest expressions of love through human contact can make everything seem all right.

Have you ever used a human touch massage chair? If you have, you know it's not anywhere close to the real thing; there is no second place to real human touch. The benefits are many: Human touch can be comforting and reassuring. Think about a time when you felt anxiety and stress, and a reassuring pat on the shoulder, simple hug, or squeeze of the hand brought you real comfort. Nonsexual human touch can lower your heart rate, reduce blood pressure, and lower stress hormone production.

If we look at the importance of a kangaroo's pouch to its young, we can see similarities to the importance of a human mother's touch and physical closeness to her child. A kangaroo's pouch is essential for the development of its young; it provides protection from harm, and keeps the young baby close to its mother's warmth, rhythm, and heartbeat. When a human baby is close to his mother, the baby is happier, and his temperature and breathing rates are more stable and more normal. Touch stimulates development of the immune system and improves emotional well-being. Touch matters throughout all of life, but is never more important than in the first year. Touch is one of the most profound ways we can tell our child that he is safe and loved.

The Benefits of Touch
Imagine going through the day without any human touch—not a hug, not a pat on the back, not even a handshake. Life would feel pretty lonely; it might even be harmful, especially to our children. A growing body of research shows that

American children and adolescents are dangerously touch-deprived. Being denied touch is a very serious problem. "Do you know what monkeys do when they are deprived of touch? They kill each other," said Tiffany Field, PhD, director of the Touch Research Institute at the University of Miami's School of Medicine. The Institute's studies have shown that touch can reduce pain and stress hormones and alleviate depression. Ms. Field continued her research on the importance of human touch by traveling to France. The people of France are known to extend more loving touch to their children than parents in any other country. She noted that young French children playing at the park were more likely to share their toys, and they were not as aggressive as their American counterparts. French parents also touched their children seven times more than what has been observed in American parents.

Not all children feel the same way about human touch. What do you do when you have a child who doesn't seem to like physical contact? Well, your child may think he doesn't enjoy loving touch, but deep down inside, he really does, and it's still vitally important to his healthy development to experience some sort of loving touch. When discussing this topic with one of my girlfriends, she told me that her young son does not enjoy snuggling, hugging, or any type of close human contact—he never has. This was challenging for her because she is a "hugging-type" person, as are her other children. She had to be creative in her approach with her son. It is routine in their household for her to visit her children's rooms before they go to sleep, tuck them in, hug and kiss them good-night, and wish them a good night's sleep. My girlfriend thought this nighttime ritual bothered her son—until he told her, "Mom, I love it when you tuck me in at night, because I sleep better when you do." Bingo! Don't ever give up; just get creative.

There have been numerous studies proving the importance of human touch to our survival. Babies need touch to thrive and grow, and this need remains with us throughout our lives. The benefits of human touch to a person's health are remarkable. Touch can reassure, relax, and comfort. It can also reduce depression, anxiety, stress, and physical pain. It increases the number of immune system cells in the body, and has powerful effects on behavior and mood. Touch is vital to a person's well-being. Humans need to touch and be touched. It is a method of communication, lifting spirits and providing an avenue for achieving happiness in life. Without it, people experience sadness, loneliness, and isolation.

Make Sure It's a Positive Touch
We can touch our children and it will stimulate love, or we can touch our children and it will stimulate fear. Pay attention to how you are touching your children, and be sure it is always an expression of love. Have you ever been going through your day and you suddenly smell something that reminds you of another time in your life? Or you might hear a song, and it will instantly trigger a memory? If I ever smell bread baking, it takes me right back to my childhood when

my mother would make homemade bread for our family every week. It is a pleasant memory of walking home from school and smelling the bread baking as I approached my house. So it is with touch. If we have a loving, positive experience with being touched, it will trigger happy memories. We will shy away from any human contact if our memory of being touched is painful and full of fear.

Researchers have found a link between the importance of touch and alleviating pain and feelings of social exclusion. One study examined how touching an inanimate object such as a teddy bear can mitigate feelings of social exclusion and poor social behavior. And this is just a teddy bear touch; think of the power behind loving human touch, like a mother's reassuring hug.

I think we would have no trouble agreeing that the discipline of a young child should be left up to the parents. Although a quick swift smack or two on the bottom will quickly stop a child from misbehaving, research now shows that the short-term response to spanking may make a child act out more in the long run. In a new study published in *Pediatrics*, researchers at Tulane University provide strong evidence that a young child who is spanked more frequently at age three will most likely become more aggressive by age five. Spanking suggests an increase in a child's aggression and violent behavior. "The reason for this may be that spanking sets up a loop of bad behavior. . . . Even if children stop tantrums when spanked, that doesn't mean they get why they shouldn't have been acting up in the first place. What's more, spanking sets a bad example, teaching children that aggressive behavior is a solution to their parents' problems," says Alice Park in *Time* magazine.

Touch not only stimulates a physical reaction, but also a form of communication. "Hesitant touch will convey uncertainty, fear and unease, while firm consistent contact signals safety, protection and love," says Tiffany Field of the Touch Research Institute. When we lovingly touch our child, it is an expression of affection and appreciation, showing that we value our child.

Our mind will create a link or anchor between a powerful feeling (love or fear) and a unique stimulus (smell, sound, or touch). If we have a negative link created in our brain, we can change that negative anchor. The way to use anchoring to transform a fear of touch to a positive emotional reaction is to select a unique stimulus (e.g., a squeeze of the hand or a pat on the shoulder)—one you control and can initiate whenever you want—and a powerful mixture of the kind of calm, confident emotions you want to experience instead of fear of being touched. Then, you simply apply this stimulus and think about a positive emotion while being touched. Your mind will literally create new neural pathways and attach them to this new, positive emotion. Now when you're touched, it will trigger a positive experience. Be sure you are touching your children in a way that will create a positive experience with human touch.

Exercises for expressing love through physical touch:

- Give your child at least one heartfelt hug every day, and watch how it will change her life.

- When standing or sitting next to your child, reach out and lovingly give him a pat or a squeeze. Acknowledge his existence.

- When walking with your child, hold her hand. The Yellow Pages got it right: "Reach out and touch someone."

- If you don't already have one, create a nighttime ritual of tucking your kids into bed. Let them know how special they are and how much they are loved, and give them a hug and a big smooch. If you are not a touchy-type family, you might want to start off small, with an affectionate, reassuring pat on the back. Figure out what feels natural for you, and keep extending that physical expression of your love.

- Some children feel uncomfortable with close physical contact. Consider creative ways to incorporate physical touch with your child; hold hands, pat him on the back, or give a high five or fist bump. A game of thumb wrestling is another fun way to incorporate physical touch.

eighteen

A conscious mother . . . has faith.

Be like the bird that, passing on her flight awhile on boughs too slight,
feels them give way beneath her,
and yet sings, knowing that she hath wings.

—VICTOR HUGO

When faced with an extreme challenge, sometimes the only thing we can control is the way we respond to the situation. Ask yourself, "Who am I going to be in the face of this? Am I going to be a woman that faces this situation with compassion and patience? Will I be a loving, caring woman who looks at this extreme challenge as an opportunity to rise to deeper levels of humanity and extend more caring and compassion? That's who I choose to be!"

Having multiple sclerosis and becoming more and more disabled, I have had to live every moment of my life with deep faith, knowing that a way will be provided for my needs to be met. I am not able to meet most of my own needs at this time, so I have to rely on others to help me. One particular morning I was really struggling; I had lost my strength and could not stand up out of my wheelchair, and my ability to breathe, speak, and swallow was also challenged. I was concerned about my fate and my lack of ability to care for myself. Although my family and friends would tell me otherwise, I was beginning to feel like a big burden to all of those around me. In my worried and troubled state, not knowing how I would care for myself and survive, I asked my husband, "How are we going to do this? How am I going to take care of myself?" His answer was perfect. "God will provide a way. That is the only answer. God will provide a way."

This has become my mantra, every moment of every day. When I'm not sure about my medication schedule, what steps I need to take to continue to heal my body, or how to meet my physical needs, I simply repeat to myself: "God will provide a way." And guess what? I am *always* completely cared for; a way is provided every time.

One morning I was struggling to get back in bed, unable to lift my legs by myself. Right at that moment, my daughter Priscilla peeked through my bedroom door and asked if I needed her help. Grateful for the offer, I said yes, and she carefully lifted my legs onto my bed. I found myself in the same situation later that same evening. Again, I was stuck, unable to get into bed. Again, Priscilla poked her sweet little head through the door and asked me if I needed help. I replied yes, and she carefully lifted my legs onto the bed. Once again, the next morning, while trying to get myself back in bed, I was unable to accomplish this task on my own.

Just at that moment Priscilla burst through the door and lovingly asked, "Mom, can I help you?" I accepted her offer as she helped me get my legs back in bed. Happy to help me, she reflected, "Wow, Mom! Look at that; whenever you need my help, I just happen to walk through the door."

God will provide a way. It has been several months since I asked my husband how I would be cared for each day, and I have to say that a way is provided, every minute of every day.

Every experience in life is part of our curriculum, designed just for us and our personal growth. Remembering this helps us to view our hardships and challenges as an opportunity for growth. Choosing to look at our lives this way requires faith. It is easy to have faith in God's infinite abundance when things are going well. It can be challenging to have this same level of belief when we cannot see the solution to the problem. Remember, everything that came into existence began from a place of being unseen first.

Can we have deep faith that our needs will be met, even when everything in front of us seems to oppose our desired outcome? In her book, *The Law of Divine Compensation*, Marianne Williamson shares an analogy that clearly illustrates the functioning of faith, and I would like to share it with you. When a pilot is flying a plane and the visibility is so poor he cannot see the horizon, does he think the horizon is gone? No. He switches the controls to autopilot. The autopilot will do for him what he cannot see and do for himself—get the plane safely to where it needs to go. And so it is with faith;

when we cannot see where we need to go, we put our life on autopilot and rely on faith. Faith can do for us what we cannot do for ourselves.

I know this to be true. Even the simplest of tasks have become challenging for me to accomplish on my own—sitting up, brushing my teeth, getting dressed, and feeding myself. I have wondered many times, "How am I going to get through the day?" The only sufficient answer is that God will provide a way. I have learned to have deep faith, knowing all that is needed will be provided. And guess what? It is!

"What the caterpillar calls the end of the world, the master calls a butterfly," Richard Bach beautifully illustrates. This is a matter of perspective. If we can hold on to the idea that our challenges are morphing us into butterflies, then we will not be like the caterpillar, thinking it is the end of the world. Have faith knowing the Master will provide a way.

Being a Model of Faith for Your Children

Deep faith is called for when everything seems to oppose what you really want in life. The choice is yours to rise up and be the exquisite woman God intended you to be. Knowing that life will supply all you need in each moment, instead of having to control the situation, just surrender and say yes! Being a model of faith for our children is a gift. As they witness through your example how to successfully and peacefully move through difficult times, everyone will learn and grow.

Being a mother is an awesome and challenging task, one that requires a great deal of patience, wisdom, and love. This tendency to worry about our children can be common. We must not allow fear and anxiety to be the guide for how we will raise our children. If we parent from fear, they will sense our apprehension and may adapt the same fearful mind-set. Make room for faith and abolish fear. There is genuine strength and power when we parent with faith and model how to live a life with deep faith, knowing all will be taken care of at the perfect time, in the perfect way. Take delight in your children; they truly are a blessing. As mothers, we are responsible for every aspect of our children: physical, financial, emotional, and spiritual. We can teach our children faith by showing them how it is lived, day in and day out.

Tough times will undoubtedly come into the lives of our children, but faith, not fear, will help them to succeed. Our children are up against more difficult challenges than when we were kids. Certainly, values have changed. We should not give in to the whims of the world. Take a stand, do not give up, protect your children, and have faith in raising them to know they will reach their highest potential. Faith is an acceptance of what we cannot see but feel deep within our heart. The dictionary defines *faith* as "believing that something is true, in spite of evidence to the contrary." Having faith and teaching our children to have faith is an important part of the fundamental growth of our relationship with our children. This will determine how they see the world. Faith will enable our child to believe in herself and live her life to its fullest potential. Exhibiting faith through our own actions with our children will show them how powerful it is to believe in things without always being able to see the physical evidence first.

Not only are we an example of faith *for* our children, but we can also demonstrate faith *in* our children. This will build their confidence. When my younger brother Dave was going through dental school, he sometimes felt overwhelmed; maybe dental school was going to be too difficult for him to complete. He told me that when he felt discouraged and wanted to quit, what kept him going was knowing that our father had faith in him. Our dad would always say, "I have faith in you; I know you can do it. Cream always rises to the top." Because Dave knew that our dad had faith in him, he ultimately had the confidence to finish dental school. Not only did my brother become a dentist, but he is also one of the best in his profession (my opinion).

Having Faith in Our Children

Most mothers have hopes, dreams, and a vision for their children. Mothers have faith in their children, knowing they have been endowed with great potential. As mothers, we hold on to that hope and faith, seeing the special unique qualities our children possess. Abraham Lincoln said, "All that I am, or hope to be, I owe to my angel mother." While Lincoln's devotion to his mother is well known, his mother was obviously devoted to her children, and had faith in Lincoln, knowing he had the potential for greatness.

Henry Ford attributes his success to his mother, stating, "I have tried to live my life as my mother would have wished.

I believe I have done, as far as I could, just what she hoped for me." His mother, Mary Litogot, had hopes and dreams for her son, always encouraging Henry's interest in machines early on. Boy, if Henry Ford hadn't been raised by a mother who had faith in his potential, the world would be a different place today. Who knows—we might still be riding horses.

Pablo Picasso knew his mother had faith in him: "When I was a child, my mother said to me, 'If you become a soldier, you'll be a general. If you become a monk, you'll end up as the Pope.' Instead, I became a painter and wound up as Picasso."

Wilma Rudolph won three gold medals at the 1960 Olympics, and was named "the fastest woman in the world." She wore metal braces on her legs as a child until she was nine years old. She said, "My doctors told me I would never walk again. My mother told me I would. I believed my mother."

A common thread among all of these famous, successful people was their high regard for their mothers, and the faith their mothers had in their potential. Have faith in your children. Their lives will reflect confidence and success simply because they knew their mother always had faith in them. You never know the impact your children may have on another's life, or even on the world, simply because of your faith in them. All children will make juvenile mistakes, immature decisions, and sometimes even be disobedient. Through loving discipline, a gentle tone, and deep faith, we can be assured that their hearts will remain sensitive and moldable as they grow into the amazing individuals they are meant to be.

Having Faith during Challenging Times

Being able to have faith in ourselves and in our future is important, especially in trying times. In a recent sermon, Pastor Joel Osteen provides a beautiful analogy regarding faith: "When you feel the storm is against you, remember, airplanes take off against the wind, not with the wind. Those winds were never meant to push you down; they are meant to lift you to a higher level of your destiny. When an eagle faces a storm, he doesn't try to fight his way through the wind, through the rain, frustrated, struggling, putting forth all this effort. No; he simply stretches out his wings and he lets the winds take him higher and higher. Finally, he rises above the storm, where it is as calm and peaceful as can be." He continues, "When the winds are blowing and things come against you, it is easy to get frustrated and start fighting and trying to change things that you were never meant to change." Have faith knowing that God is in control of the storm. Then, when the winds and the storms arrive, and it seems like they are pushing you down, you will know that they are in your life for a reason, lifting you higher and higher. "God wouldn't have allowed the storm if it were going to keep you from your destiny," says Pastor Osteen. Faith is when you meet a limited circumstance with unlimited thinking. Knowing I am a child of God, I know that everything is going to be all right.

Early one morning while reading, I came across a quote from the *Tao Te Ching* that has stuck with me:

Fire cools

Water seeks its own level

This means that no matter how extreme the situation, it will change. The forest fire *always* burns itself out. That is why even in the midst of an extreme situation, the wise are patient. They know that healing will follow the upheaval. *A Course in Miracles* states, "Those who are certain of the outcome can afford to wait, and wait without anxiety." Now that is unwavering faith!

"When faith in love and its miraculous authority becomes a thought form that guides our thinking, it turns into an extraordinary power that transforms our lives," suggests Marianne Williamson in her book, *The Law of Divine Compensation.* It is not enough that spiritual power exists; we must have faith that it exists to be able to put this spiritual power in motion. We have heard that "Faith is blind." Faith is not blind; faith is visionary, Marianne imparts. Sometimes life seems so difficult, and we cannot see a positive solution. How am I going to pay the bills, cope with the bad medical report, address trouble with my children . . . ? If we have faith in a positive outcome, we are not being delusional; it simply means that we are affirming a solution. Faith enables us to see beyond what is happening and see what could be happening.

There are six children in my family. When I was fourteen years old, two weeks before I was beginning my freshman year of high school, my three sisters were in a horrible, life-threatening car accident. They each had multiple injuries, including internal bleeding, collapsed lungs, and broken bones, and all three were in a coma. The doctors did not expect any of them to survive. Preparing my parents for the inevitable outcome, the doctors stated that if they did survive, they would never fully recover, leading difficult lives with major disabilities. Although upset, distressed, worried, and saddened, I witnessed my parents holding on to their faith. As they went from one hospital room to the next and from one surgery to the next, meeting with doctor after doctor after doctor, they moved about the hospital with confidence and peace in their hearts, having deep faith, knowing all would be well. My parents were great examples of faith for my siblings and me, believing that something is true in spite of evidence to the contrary. Much to the surprise of the doctors, each one of my sisters did recover completely, and they went on to lead very full, extraordinary lives.

As mothers, our actions create the daily impact that establishes the mind-set of our children. Guiding our children to have faith in their unique potential cultivates conviction, and is the initial step in being able to act upon it. By reciting daily affirmations of confidence to your children, examining choices that they create, both positive and negative, and encouraging them to use their resourcefulness to move upon constructive thoughts, you will help them to believe in themselves and inspire them to give their best.

Trusting our children to make the proper decisions with our direction gives them the freedom to develop their own faith, and leads them to make the right choices. This is the beginning of teaching faith. Inspiring faith in our children as a belief system as they become young adults is vital, because it promotes self-confidence, even when they are unsuccessful at something.

Exercises for increasing faith:

- When faced with a difficult situation, ask yourself, "Who am I going to be in the face of this challenge? What can I be responsible for?" Then show up with courage and deep faith.

- Breathe slowly and deeply, knowing that God is co-creating your life with you, that He wants you to flourish, and that He will support you daily with all that you need.

- Look at your child. See your child. Have hope and faith in the potential of your child. Know he is here for greatness. Be sure you remember to verbalize this to your child. He will become great, because you know he is great.

- Are you having a challenge in your life? This seems like a silly question, I know. Look at your challenge as an opportunity for growth. "If you don't like something, change it. If you can't change it, change your attitude," advises Maya Angelou.

- Repeat words of affirmation to your children daily. This will build their confidence and teach them to have faith in their own ability to be successful.

nineteen

A conscious mother . . .
loves unconditionally.

Someday, after mastering the winds, the waves, the tides, and gravity, we shall harness for God the energies of love, and then, for a second time in the history of the world, man will have discovered fire.

—PIERRE TEILHARD DE CHARDIN

Unconditional love is known as affection without limitations. Most will agree that unconditional love is the type of love that has no limits or restrictions; it is unchanging. Unconditional love will encourage security, joy, strength, courage, and happiness. Love is unconditional when it endures despite unfavorable circumstances. When preparing and researching for this chapter, I had a sudden awareness that I have been blessed to be the recipient of numerous acts of unconditional love. My husband and my children have continually cared for me and loved me despite undesirable circumstances. This is the measure of love and care that we should demonstrate to our children.

As I came to write the final chapter of this book, I noticed that I felt exhausted, like I'd "hit the wall," so to speak. Although I find the topic of unconditional love to be of the utmost importance, I also find it extremely difficult to put into words. To demonstrate unconditional love to our children, we must first exhibit unconditional love for ourselves. There are four distinct words in Greek for love: *agape, eros, philia,* and *storge. Agape* means love in a "spiritual" sense; it often refers to a general endearment or deeper sense of true unconditional love. This type of love is selfless; it gives without expecting anything in return. Whether the love given is returned or not, the person continues to give, even without self-benefit. Agape love is also used to indicate the feelings a parent may have for their children. Agape love is unconditional love. For this chapter, we focus on agape love.

I love the fall. It's my favorite season of the year, bringing cool weather, the beautiful colors of changing leaves, and a warm fire in the fireplace. One fall day I was out running errands, and a vibrant red leaf caught my eye. What I experienced next changed the way I understand love. It is difficult to convey this experience and be fully accurate. When I saw the leaf, I experienced real, genuine love. It was pure. The "love energy" from the leaf and myself became one. This profound experience truly changed me. I felt overwhelming love . . . in a leaf! The love energy I experienced was oneness. I could not define where my love began; it was all from the same source. If I can have this kind of experience in nature, think of the strong feelings of love I can exchange with my husband, children, other family members, and friends.

A couple of weeks later, I was enjoying lunch at a local deli with my three youngest daughters. Sitting at the table next to me was an older woman. She adored my children, and we started to visit.

"Enjoy them while they are young, and don't blink," she said. "It goes by so fast." She told me that her children were all grown, and that she'd been married to the love of her life for almost sixty years. He now had Alzheimer's disease, and she was his caregiver. Although it was difficult, she was able to take a break from caring for him now and then, and enjoy a lunch out, as she was doing that day. I looked at the older woman's face while we chatted, and I felt the same exchange of "love energy" that I'd experienced with the beautiful red leaf. I saw myself in the older woman's eyes. What was happening? I was having these experiences of feeling connected to others, and experiencing unconditional love for myself and everyone and everything around me. It was perfect. These experiences have provided me with a barometer of sorts, by which to measure the feelings of love I extend to others in my life, especially my children.

One of my favorite gifts to receive is a heartfelt love note. My husband wrote a special note to me one Mother's Day. He expressed so clearly the importance of a mother's love:

I have always felt that the closest love we feel in this life, which is like God's love, is a mother's love. Everyone who is born has a mother, and God made it so—so we would not feel far from our heavenly home. I remember when I was three years old, looking up at my mother's eyes and wondering, "Who is this kind and loving creature that takes care of me?"

We all need to feel this kind of love in our lives, and we can extend this God-like love to our children. Ralph Waldo Emerson once said, "Men are what their mothers made them." The same is true for women, who typically grow up to become similar to their mothers. There is something about a mother's love and care that shapes us into the unique person we will eventually grow to become.

The Greatest Gift We Can Give Our Children—Unconditional Love for Oneself

The greatest single gift we can give our children is to love ourselves and work on ourselves. Our DNA, our characteristics, our temperament, and some of our habits and patterns are given to us by our parents and our parents' parents. We can also pass along to our children the gift of "I will consciously transform myself." Mothering ourselves is the first step to raising our children. We have been so conditioned to look outside of ourselves for external changes to make our inner world feel more at peace. It is our inner world that needs our attention, care, nurturing, loving heart, embrace, and tender touch. Going within to learn to love all aspects of ourselves is the most powerful transformative tool we can employ, and one that will have profound effects on the external world around us.

Each and every day, mothers wake up deeply desiring to be the best we can be for our children. We want to do all we intuitively know how to do; we want to be exactly as we know how to be; and we want to be that model for our children. However, one crazy morning trying to get out the door on time, another crash of orange juice on the floor, more bills piling up, or a strained marriage stemming from the unending pressures of family life, and by three p.m. we have fallen back into a habitual way of being. We lapse into autopilot mode, falling back on patterns found in an older part of our brain. We open our mouths and out comes an expression from our mother or father—and not the most gracious parts of their personalities, but the parts of them we swore we would never emulate.

Most of us have been raised, through no fault of our own, or of our parents, to use fear as the primary mode of discipline. We manipulate, we threaten, and we punish. In her book, *Conscious Discipline*, Becky Bailey talks about discipline that has relied on fear. Fear of punishment might look like a spanking; fear of loss of love may sound like "I am so disappointed in you"; fear of failure resonates in the statement "Is it too much to ask?"; fear of abandonment echoes in the threat "Get in the car or I'm leaving." There are consequences when we rely on fear to discipline. We are focusing on what we *don't* want. As Becky Bailey so comically states, "It is as if we walk around following our children with a highlighter; oops, pick up your socks or no TV; oops, finish your dinner or no dessert; oops, practice harder or you are not going to make the competitive squad; oops, you spilt the milk again." We highlight all of the errors, and it turns into a self-perpetuating belief that we are not good enough.

Listen to your own inner voice to see if you can hear that inner critic using fear to motivate. When you try to motivate yourself, do you hear, "Work out all week, and you can have one night out at a restaurant," or "Get to the gym or you won't look good in that new dress"? This harsh inner critic is playing a constant recording of all the ways we are not good enough. We tend to instill the same type of inner critic motivated by fear in our children. Usually, after we are overly critical with our children, we end up overcompensating the other way by pouring on the praise: "Good job! You scored a goal!" "Excellent—you colored that picture so well!" "Amazing work—you got all A's, and you deserve some money." We overcompensate by telling ourselves, "Forget it; I'm buying that new skirt." "I don't care how I look—I'm going to have seconds." "I'm going to just ignore the bills because I don't know how to handle them." We swing between yo-yo thinking, from scarcity to plenty, from harsh criticism to over-compensation, from eating too much to eating too little.

This is where the inner work on self comes in. It is time to become conscious of our deepest desires and our needs, and to soothe and contain our own inner child, who has false beliefs and feels that she is not good enough, not worthy, not visible. We can practice our conscious parenting skills on ourselves first before we practice them on our children. We will begin to transform our own lives and stop ourselves from imparting the same false beliefs to our children. The brain works best when one feels safe. If we do not feel safe, then we will easily fall back into the routine patterns familiar to our brain.

Give Your Children the Gift of Unconditional Love

A mother's love for her children is infinite and limitless. Mothers continually love their children, even though they may have flaws and imperfections.

Dr. Eben Alexander, MD, had a fascinating near-death experience when he contracted meningitis. In his book, *Proof of Heaven,* he reveals the feeling of unconditional love he felt in this spiritual realm, explaining, "You are loved and cherished, dearly, forever. You have nothing to fear. There is nothing you can do wrong [in this realm]." When we experience pure love to this degree, it transcends all else. Love your children unconditionally. Nurture them and care for them. Help your children to know that they are loved completely, just the way they are.

After raising six happy, compassionate, loving, successful children, my mother was asked, "How did you do it?" Her reply: "If your children feel they are loved, then you have won half the battle." If a child grows up knowing he is loved, this will foster a sense of worthiness, instilling the belief in the child that he is worthy of all good things. "You practice loving God by loving another human," suggests author and film producer Olivia Harrison.

If I had to select one concept in this whole book that I believe is the most important foundation upon which to raise a child, it would be this: Our children need to know they are deeply loved, completely, just the way they are . . . unconditional love. When we are in the presence of our children and they feel our unconditional love for them, it is powerful. This kind of love can change your heart. And when you know what changes the heart, you know what changes the world. It starts with loving our children. The currency of love is attention. We need to give our children the attention they so desperately desire.

When parenting our children, we should allow them to figure out the direction of their lives without interjecting our own personal agenda. One conscious mother has a sixteen-year-old daughter, Gabrielle, who is trying to figure out what she wants to do with her life this year. Gabrielle spent the past school year in France as a foreign exchange student, and now doesn't feel like she fits in at home, or at school. She would like to explore the option of moving to Canada to live with her aunt and finish high school there. Her mother has decided to parent her daughter the way she would like to be parented. She is extending guidance, confidence, and deep love as her daughter sorts through the many options before her.

Unfortunately, most children do not get enough unconditional love. When children behave well and are pristine, silent, and obedient, they often experience signs of our validation and acceptance—a smile, our tender nature, kind words. But they experience the ramifications of conditional love when they are noisy, wayward, troublesome, and otherwise inconvenient. The smiles and kind words vanish instantly, and from our reactions they receive this message: "When you are good, I love you, but when you are not, I don't." This is the worst blow a child can experience, and the ramifications are far-reaching. In his book *Real Love*, Greg Baer, MD, explains, "All of our children's behaviors that we find exasperating—anger, defiance, fighting with their siblings, withdrawal, lying, lack of responsibility, and so on—are nothing more than reactions to not feeling a sufficient supply of one thing: real love. Real love is as essential to their emotional health as air, water, and food are to their physical well-being."

Recently, my aunt shared a beautiful story about how simple it can be to love. She has ten children, and during this particular time period, half of them were teenagers and the other half were young children. She was being challenged by one of her teenage sons. It seemed that the trouble was never-ending. A stream of phone calls flooded her home, with calls coming in from friends, schoolteachers, neighborhood parents, youth church leaders, and, occasionally, the local police, complaining of this child's poor behavior.

After receiving yet another phone call expressing disapproval for her son's actions, she hung up the phone, and, with a heavy sigh and sheer frustration, she mumbled the question, "What am I going to do with that kid?" Unbeknownst to my aunt, her three-year-old son was standing right behind her, listening in on the conversation. He had a simple answer to her question: "Mom, all you have to do is just pick him up and love him." This little three-year-old was quite insightful. It has often been said, "From the mouths of babes . . ."

As this three-year-old boy grew up to be a young man, he would bring his friends over to his house to hang out. Sometimes these friends were not the most stellar of people, and they would feel a bit uncomfortable coming in to meet my aunt and uncle. My cousin was quick to reassure them, saying, "My mom and dad are not going to judge you; they will love you." He knew that no matter what, unconditional love was extended in their home. When our children feel this level of acceptance, respect, value, and love for self, they will grow up accepting, respecting, valuing, and loving themselves and others.

You Can Express Unconditional Love and Still Discipline Your Child

Another way to show love for our children is through discipline and by setting boundaries. Some parents have a difficult time disciplining their children because they feel that their children won't like them afterward, or that their children might feel unloved. It is *because* we love our children that we discipline them and set boundaries. We may have to reprimand them, but when it is done out of love, our children will feel safe and know they can come to us for anything. We will always be there for them. As parents, it is vitally important that we set boundaries to ensure the proper growth and development of our children. When boundaries are set, it has an enormous impact on their self-esteem, how they develop morals, and how well they will do academically, socially, and in relationships.

According to Native American tradition, the Plains Indians believe the sun has great power because it gives the Earth warmth and light. The sun rises every day and shines its light on us all, asking nothing in return. The Earth is believed to be the mother of all things because of its nurturance. Without the sun there would be no growth, and without the Earth it would be impossible to foster maturation. When we look at disciplining our children, there must be a beautiful balance between the sun/heat and the earth/encouraging. Setting boundaries may feel like the heat coming down from the sun, but without that heat, our children would not grow. When we combine that with nurturing encouragement, our children have a place to sprout and bloom.

In Dr. Henry Cloud and Dr. John Townsend's book, *Boundaries*, they outline five needs that positive boundary setting addresses for children:

1. Self-protection. It is important to set boundaries to keep our children safe. Boundaries keep them away from things that can be harmful, and will keep things that are healthy for them close by.

2. Taking responsibility for one's own needs. One of the most important things a mother can do is to encourage in her child the expression of feelings, even if it does not match the feelings of the rest of the family, or anyone else. Allow your children to express their negative emotions, and, most important, don't try to fix things for them. They will naturally learn to validate and trust their own feelings.

3. Having a sense of control and choice. Whether it is allowing your child to choose what they would like to eat for breakfast or which college they would like to apply to, children like to feel they are in control and have a say in the matter. This will allow our children to feel empowered rather than helpless and dependent upon others. When disciplining our children, we can also help them to feel a sense of control and choice. For example, when a child refuses to clean her room, we can say, "By choosing not to clean your room, you are also choosing to not go out with your friends this weekend." This type of loving discipline will help our children understand that every choice has a consequence.

4. Delaying gratification. When we teach our children the importance of delaying gratification, we teach them the value of saving, the value of patience, and the value of waiting their turn. We can start teaching this at a very young age, keeping them from turning into adults with an "I want it now" attitude. This also teaches our children the value of hard work, to be more goal-oriented, and to value what they buy.

5. Respecting the limits of others. Kids by nature are egocentric and think the world revolves around them. Boundaries help them to realize that the world does not revolve around them. This is important, because it teaches our children that when they hear the word "no," they need to listen and respect it. It also teaches our children to have empathy for another's limits and needs. They will learn to think about how other people feel, not just how they feel.

You can see the important benefits of loving discipline and setting boundaries. Our children may not enjoy it in the moment, but setting boundaries and ensuring loving discipline are some of the greatest expressions of love we can ever extend to our children. Unconditional love means caring about another person without expecting anything in return. So, when our children misbehave, we must continue to love and accept them completely. This can be tricky, but it is imperative that we continue to express unconditional love even when our children do not respond well to the disciplinary actions we have put in place. Love your child even if you do not love his conduct. In order to be happy, children just need to feel loved.

Exercises for expressing unconditional love:

- Simply extend love to your children. Help them to feel valued and loved completely, just the way they are.

- Remember the "Golden Rule"? *Do unto others as you would have them do unto you.* Try to practice this in your own life as you teach your children to embrace it.

- Treat your children with the same love and respect you desire to have in your own life. Think about what you say and how you are saying it, before you speak.

- Take some time to be in nature. Look—really *look* at a flower, a leaf, a tree, or the sky. All things were created for our enjoyment. Can you see the indescribable beauty? Can you feel God's immense love for you? You are His greatest creation.

- A great way to assess boundary setting for our children is to ask ourselves, "Would I do these things myself?" We will have a much easier time teaching our children the importance of setting boundaries if we are practicing what we preach.

acknowledgments

After observing my interactions with my children, a new friend commented, "You've got a book in you." I thought to myself, "Yes! I *do* have a book in me." She continued, "You are such a good mother, and there's a lot of love in your family. You have to write a book about being a successful mother." From that night on, and every night that followed for the next four weeks, I would wake up at 4:04 in the morning, inspired to write what would become *The Essence of a Mother*. Stacy Prillaman, thank you for the beautiful idea.

I have the utmost appreciation for my children, Scott, McKenna, Abigail, Priscilla, and Lola. Scott, thank you for helping me type when my fingers were too tired, and thank you for your creative mind in helping me with edits. McKenna, thank you for stepping up and running errands while I was writing. Abi, thank you for helping your little sister feel special, and Priscilla, thank you for helping to cook all of those delicious meals so I could work on my book. Lola, thank you for being patient, entertaining yourself, and giving me quiet time to write. To all of you, thank you for the selfless service you give me every single day—I know it is not easy. Without my children, this book would not exist. I have learned about and practiced being a conscious mother from all of you. It is an honor to be your mother.

Thank you to my beautiful mother, Shayne McCook. I would never have been capable of writing this book if I had not been mothered well. Your example of patience and unconditional love is profoundly appreciated. I stand on the shoulders of all of the loving and gracious women, grandmothers, great-grandmothers, and aunts who came before me. It is because of your strength and courage to be conscious women and mothers that I am the mother and woman I am today.

To my husband, Chris—I am deeply grateful for your inexhaustible help, undying love, and unlimited support . . . come what may. You give meaning to the marriage vows "for better or worse, in sickness and in health." I could never have gotten this far without you. Also, thank you for snoring; it kept me awake in the middle of the night, giving me plenty of time to write.

I also want to thank my sisters for brainstorming with me during times when I was stuck.

I extend my deep gratitude to Micheline Green. Thank you for encouraging, pushing, and stretching me to be vulnerable and more transparent in my writing. I appreciate your input and all of your support.

Linda Sivertsen, thank you for your support and inspiration in creating my *Big, Beautiful Book Proposal*. You are the "book mama." Laura Yorke, my literary agent, thank you for getting my book read and helping me to land a publishing deal. Many thanks to Lara Asher for your thoughtful input and edits. You have been instrumental in making this book a reality.

And many thanks to the numerous angel-friends who support me and my family with compassion, generosity, and kindness. Thank you for grocery shopping, cooking meals, driving the kids around, stopping by, calling just to chat, or simply giving hugs.

about the author

Julie S. Jensen is a forty-four-year-old mother of five with over twenty-two years of real-life experience in the most important role on Earth: raising children. At first, she was just like every other mother, exhausted by trying to keep up with the many activities of her children. But multiple sclerosis forced her to slow down and really consider how and where to spend her limited energy. It forced her to look inside and ask: *Is my value just my physical body—my ability to do, and to be productive?* The answer is no. She realized that the true source of her value and power comes from within, and with that understanding, she knew she had to teach this simple truth—and others—to her children. Julie has also developed the Global Shared Agreements Program for young girls, a self-empowerment program designed to positively shift the culture of girls. It has now been adopted by teachers and guidance counselors. She wrote a curriculum and began a course to train more teachers to use the program in the public school system. A fourteen-week pilot program for Global Shared Agreements for Schools began January 2013 in one school in Arizona. This program was selected by the participants at the Awakened World Peace Summit as an initiative they will support and promote on a global scale. She is co-founder of The Essence Foundation, a nonprofit public charity, providing transformative learning products and programs designed for Mothers, Teachers, and Girls. Julie resides in Northern California with her husband, Chris, and their five children. You can visit Julie at her website, www.pure-essence.org.